NAPOLEON HILL  IS ON THE AIR!

THE FIVE FOUNDATIONS FOR SUCCESS

NAPOLEON HILL IS ON THE AIR!

Never Before Published

RADIO BROADCASTS

with Napoleon Hill

GRAND HARBOR PRESS

Published by Grand Harbor Press, Grand Haven, MI

www.brilliancepublishing.com

Amazon, the Amazon logo, and Grand Harbor Press are trademarks of Amazon.com, Inc., or its affiliates.

ISBN-13: 9781503942912
ISBN-10: 1503942910

Cover design by Faceout Studio

Printed in the United States of America

CONTENTS

EDITOR'S NOTE

In 1883, in the mountains of Wise County in southwest Virginia, Oliver Napoleon Hill was born into poverty. His father, James, was a jack-of-all-trades, and little is known about his mother, Sara, who died when Napoleon was nine years old. The eldest of two sons from his parents' marriage, Napoleon was named after a rich uncle to gain favor and, hopefully, an inheritance. That plan didn't work, but Napoleon would eventually discover his own riches, financial and otherwise.

Growing up, Napoleon Hill was a wild young man, known for carrying his six-shooter with him every chance he got, just like his hero, the outlaw Jesse James. He had very little education and few material advantages, later describing Wise County as famous for three things: moonshine, feuding, and ignorant people.

At ten years old, Napoleon's direction in life changed when his father remarried. An educated and refined woman, his stepmother, Martha Ramey Banner, soon had Napoleon attending church and buckling down in school. She convinced him to trade his six-shooter for a typewriter and encouraged him to write. He followed her advice and discovered he had a talent. He would go on to become one of the most widely read authors in the world.

While working as a reporter for *Bob Taylor's Magazine* in 1908, Napoleon was assigned to interview the steel magnate Andrew Carnegie. Mr. Carnegie, founder of U.S. Steel Corporation, took an immediate liking to Napoleon and, after three days of interviews, made him an offer that would completely change his life. Mr. Carnegie said he would introduce Napoleon to the most successful men in America if Hill would spend up to twenty years, without pay, distilling and compiling from these interviews the first-ever written philosophy of success.

During those twenty years Napoleon also operated a number of businesses, some successful, some not. He was an executive at a gas company, owned a candy company, and taught in business and correspondence colleges. He published two motivational magazines, *Hill's Golden Rule* and *Napoleon Hill's Magazine*, and, with introductions from Andrew Carnegie in hand, he met and interviewed hundreds of the most successful men of his day, including Thomas Edison, Henry Ford, Dr. Alexander Graham Bell, F. W. Woolworth, Harvey Firestone of the Firestone Tire and Rubber Company, and John Wanamaker.

In 1928, after Napoleon had completed his twenty-year task, he published the eight-volume work *The Law of Success.* In 1937, amid the Great Depression, he published a condensed version of that work, which he called *Think and Grow Rich.* Now recognized as one of the bestselling and most influential motivational books written, *Think and Grow Rich* has been translated into more than forty languages and has influenced hundreds of millions of people throughout the world.

Napoleon Hill went on to write many more motivational books, including *The Magic Ladder to Success, How to Sell Your Way through Life, The Master Key to Riches,* and *How to Raise Your Own Salary.* He served as an adviser to two presidents, Woodrow Wilson and Franklin D. Roosevelt and, during the 1930s and 1940s, continued his educational businesses and lectured widely.

In 1941, Dr. William Plumer Jacobs II, president of the Presbyterian College in Clinton, South Carolina, brought Napoleon to Clinton to write *Mental Dynamite,* booklets that covered the seventeen success principles Napoleon had discovered. Nearly ten years later, Napoleon settled happily into semiretirement. But in 1952, while delivering a speech to the Rotary Club in Chicago, he met W. Clement Stone, a wealthy insurance man. Mr. Stone had given away thousands of copies of *Think and Grow Rich* over the years, and he believed so fervently in the principles of success that he coaxed Napoleon out of retirement. Together they went on to offer courses based on the success principles and wrote the bestselling book *Success through a Positive Mental Attitude*.

In 1953, a year after teaming up with Napoleon Hill, Mr. Stone arranged for him to present a series of radio broadcasts on a local radio station in Jackson, Mississippi, in the hopes it would help the people of that city achieve greater success. These broadcasts were well received, and Napoleon would continue to conduct radio and television shows in other cities throughout the United States until his death in 1970.

The book you're about to read contains the transcripts from that series of Jackson radio programs that Napoleon Hill launched in 1953. It allows you, the reader, to experience almost verbatim what Napoleon shared directly with his listeners.

In these broadcasts, he highlights what he called the "Big Five" of the seventeen distinct principles of success—Definiteness of Purpose, the Mastermind, Applied Faith, Going the Extra Mile, and Creative Vision—and includes examples of how these five principles have led some famous and not-so-famous people to success. He also includes a number of clues about his single most important success principle. Napoleon never told the world what that principle was, not in these broadcasts or anywhere else, leaving his readers and listeners to discover it for themselves. But he said many times that when his followers were ready, they would discover what he called "The Supreme Secret of Personal Achievement."

Perhaps you will be ready to discover it as you read these never-before-published broadcasts.

INTRODUCTION

I am a medical doctor living in Conway, South Carolina, and enjoying my ninth decade of life. I am also the chairman of the Napoleon Hill Foundation and the nephew of its famous namesake. So I was thrilled when Grand Harbor Press asked me to provide some memories of growing up with my remarkable uncle Nap, to be used as an introduction to this book.

When I was very young, my parents divorced, and my mother and I moved in with my unmarried aunt, Annie Lou Norman, in Clinton, South Carolina. Annie Lou had a responsible job at the W. P. Jacobs Company, a large publishing firm owned by Dr. William Plumer Jacobs, who also served as president of Presbyterian College in Clinton. As she was on her own and busy with work, she needed someone to keep house for her. In return for this service, she offered to support my mother, who at the time had no other skills with which to support her family, namely me.

We weren't the only ones Aunt Annie Lou looked after. Another sister, my aunt Mary, also moved in, along with her two daughters, Patricia and Mary Ruth, and, to my great dismay, their two female dogs. It was quite distressing to me that I was the only male in that big three-story house. My only interaction with father figures was through some of my friends' fathers, who kindly took me fishing and hunting. Then one day, Annie Lou took in another boarder, a gentleman brought to Clinton by

Dr. Jacobs to write a series of motivational books and present lectures. He was, of course, Napoleon Hill.

By then, Mr. Hill was a very successful man, having written *Think and Grow Rich* four years earlier, though I was too young to be aware of this at the time. He was also a busy man, spending his days writing on the third floor of my aunt's house and his nights lecturing at various locations. I recall little interaction with him at first, other than his scolding me for tampering with the radio on a nice Sunday afternoon in December of 1941. It was the day of the attack on Pearl Harbor, and he of course wanted to listen to the news, while I wanted to hear the comic strips read, a common Sunday radio program at the time. Still, I was quite impressed that he had a great interest in and knowledge of what was going on in the world. From then on, he devoted a good deal of time to teaching me about world affairs, and I was fascinated to sit at his knee and listen.

After Mr. Hill moved in, I recall rummaging in a closet and finding a number of books wrapped up in paper. Naturally, I tore into them to see if they contained anything I would be interested in. These were booklets that Dr. Jacobs had encouraged Napoleon to write about the principles of personal achievement. I found two booklets that I became particularly intrigued with. One was about Definiteness of Purpose and the other focused on Going the Extra Mile, which, to this day, is my favorite principle. I read and reread the booklets on these two timeless success principles, which are among the Five Foundations for Success featured in the book you are about to read.

Napoleon and Annie Lou became friends and soon began courting. Napoleon had a very strange automobile called a DeSoto, with a long hood and a much longer trunk. Two people could comfortably sit in the front, and that was where Napoleon and his sweetheart, my aunt, sat whenever we took a drive. There was a small space behind the front seats that he had redone, and we all thought it was intended as tiny seats for family members. We were wrong. Napoleon had fixed up these seats for his two Pomeranian dogs, Little Girl and Big Boy. On weekend out-ings, we would all get in the trunk and on the running boards—me, my mother, Aunt Mary, my two cousins, and their two female dogs—while Napoleon's two dogs rode up front. Nonetheless, we all enjoyed these trips, because, for the first time, we had access to an automobile.

Napoleon had a soft spot in his heart for those dogs, but he cared for his adopted family as well. My mother and Annie Lou attended his lectures, and Mother was inspired by them to go to school and earn a degree in accounting. Annie Lou was romantically inspired, and she and Napoleon married in December of 1943. They lived happily ever after.

Meanwhile, I was growing into my teenage years and had developed an interest in eventually studying medicine. Even with my mother's new position as an accountant, though, medical school was clearly beyond our financial means. It seemed like just a dream.

And so, around 1956, after graduating from college, I applied to the US Air Force to become a pilot. This was quite an ambitious goal, as I had never even been in an airplane, but Uncle Nap always said that I could do whatever I set out to do, so long as I believed I could and acted on it. I remember quite vividly going to Valdosta, Georgia, and being tested extensively to become an aviation cadet. I passed all the mental, psychological, and physical tests. But on a very hot, humid Georgia day, I experienced some wheezing, which ended my air force career before it started. An air force physician feared that using oxygen in an airplane would make my asthma much worse. I'd had a purpose and I'd acted on it. Only ill health stopped me from achieving my goal.

Deterred from my air force ambition, I found that my desire to go to medical school was rekindled. But how could I achieve my goal?

Napoleon's work in Clinton had long since concluded. He and his new wife, Annie Lou, had moved to bustling California, where he lectured and taught his success principles on radio broadcasts, motiva-tional programs similar to those that appear in this book. He could have forgotten the sisters-in-law and nephew he left behind, but he didn't.

He came to my rescue by offering to lend me all the money I needed to attend medical school. I eagerly took him up on that offer and devoted myself to my definite major purpose, going the extra mile to achieve my medical degree in 1960. I am grateful to Uncle Nap to this day, as I'm still enjoying practicing medicine. I couldn't have done it without him.

Reading through the Five Foundations for Success presented in this book has brought Uncle Nap back to life for me. My two favorite success principles—Definiteness of Purpose and Going the Extra Mile—as well as the Mastermind, Applied Faith, and Creative Vision, were frequent subjects of discussion in our parlor in Clinton, discussions that helped direct this young boy's life. Reading this never-before-published book, I imagined myself sitting at my uncle's knee once more.

Napoleon Hill was like a father to me, and his success principles have guided me throughout my life. I believe you, too, will be motivated to achieve success and happiness by reading, studying, and enjoying his teachings.

Dr. Charles Winfield Johnson
Conway, South Carolina
December 2016

ONE
GREETINGS

Dr. Hill:

Greetings, my friends. May I tell you the strange story of the force now being let loose in the world that may well bring peace of mind and material success to you and all your loved ones? The story began in a one-room log cabin in the mountains of Virginia over fifty years ago, where I first saw the light of day. My only inheritance at birth was poverty, ignorance, fear, and superstition. And theoretically, I hadn't the slightest reason to hope that I might ever be of service to mankind, but the arm of fate is very long and the hand of destiny is very strong, and somehow this great arm reached into the wilderness where I was born and led me out to render a service to mankind that may well become the foundation on which will rest all peaceful and successful human relations.

The Meanest Boy in Wise County

Commentator:

Dr. Hill, did you recognize when you were very young that you were destined to give the world its practical philosophy of personal success?

Or just when did you first recognize that you were blessed with this privilege?

Dr. Hill:

I hadn't the slightest idea what my lot in life was to be until I was nine years of age and my father brought home my new mother after my own mother had passed on. Up to that time, my greatest ambition was to become a second Jesse James with enough devilishness in me to enable me to outdo the original Jesse.

Commentator:

Well then, something must have happened to have caused you to change your major purpose in life, and I am sure our radio audience would like to hear what it was.

Dr. Hill:

Yes, something did happen which changed my aim in life. It happened when I was introduced to my stepmother, and she made a one-sentence speech that was destined not only to change my life, but through me it was to change the lives of millions of people throughout the world—some of them not yet born. After my father had introduced my step-mother to all the other relatives that had come to our house to meet her, he came around to me. I was standing over in the corner of the room with my arms folded and looking as tough as I possibly could and all set to hate that woman who had come to take my mother's place. My father gave me an astounding introduction by saying, "Martha, this is your son Napoleon, the meanest boy in Wise County, and I shouldn't be surprised if he starts throwing rocks at you by tomorrow morning."

Commentator:

Well, that was quite a dramatic introduction. What did your step-mother have to say about it?

Dr. Hill:

Well, she walked over to me, lifted my chin with her hand, looked me squarely in the eyes for a few moments, then turned to my father and delivered a speech that made him cringe and reached deeply into my very own soul. "You are dead wrong about this boy," she exclaimed. "He is not the meanest boy in Wise County, but the smartest boy who hasn't yet learned how to direct his smartness." Well, that was the most thrilling moment of my life because it was the first time anyone had ever said anything kind about me, and somehow I had a sort of premonition that a new soul had been born within me. That short speech made a profound impression on my father also, and I saw my relatives gasp with astonishment when they heard my stepmother.

Andrew Carnegie's Motive

Commentator:

Did you recognize then that you were destined to project your influence throughout the world?

Dr. Hill:

No. It was several years later, when I was in my twenties, that I discovered I was being favored by the circumstances of my life far beyond that to which my age and experience entitled me. Through my stepmother's direction I had become a news writer for small country papers and had acquired considerable ability to dramatize news stories. This ability got me my first interview with the late Andrew Carnegie, and it was he who discovered that I had the inherent qualities he considered essential for a job that would require twenty years of unpaid research in the organization of a successful philosophy based on the know-how of men who had learned the principles of success from a lifetime of experience informed by the trial-and-error method.

Commentator:

Dr. Hill, what was Andrew Carnegie's motive in wanting you to organize a success philosophy?

Dr. Hill:

Mr. Carnegie believed it was a great economic waste for men and women to have to spend a lifetime learning the way to success when they might easily acquire this information in a few weeks by studying the experiences of men who had learned the long hard way.

Commentator:

Do you believe, Dr. Hill, that the students of your philosophy have as great a chance to become financially independent now as the successful men who helped you organize this success principle?

Dr. Hill:

The assumption that opportunities are fewer today than they were when men like Henry Ford and Thomas A. Edison began their careers is false and unsound, because the whole world is demanding a new group of pioneers with the capacity to conceive new ideas, new inventions, and better ways of living together peacefully.

Practical Dreamers

Commentator:

Do you feel, Dr. Hill, that your success philosophy is a means by which new leaders may find these opportunities in all walks of life?

Dr. Hill:

The science of success inspires men and women to become practical dreamers who rise above unfriendly circumstances and create their own opportunities to fit their own aims and ambitions. Practical dreamers have always been the pattern makers of civilization, and they always will be. Any person who in the future cherishes a lofty dream and holds fast to it will be more than apt to see that dream become a reality, for truly this is an age that needs practical dreamers.

Well, come now and let us turn back the pages of history and revisit some of the practical dreamers who gave us the civilization and the way of life we now enjoy. For example, Columbus dreamed of an unknown world and discovered it. He discovered it through the application of some of the selfsame principles that have brought success to so many of my students, such as the principle of Definiteness of Purpose, the habit of Going the Extra Mile, and Applied Faith.

Henry Ford dreamed of a horseless carriage, and, despite his poverty, he made his dream come true and belted the entire earth with his automobile. Well, Ford was both a student of my success philosophy and a collaborator in its development. Thomas A. Edison dreamed of an electric lamp, lighted by electricity, and lived through more than ten thousand different failures before he was crowned by success. He, too, helped me to give the world its first practical philosophy of personal success. And the Wright brothers dreamed of a machine that would fly, and they carried that dream to success through the application of my success philosophy. Guglielmo Marconi dreamed of a system for harnessing the ether and using it for communication without the aid of wires. Through the application of my philosophy, he made that dream come true.

All these great achievements were at first nothing but the nebulous emotions of a dreamer, but they were transmuted into reality by the application of a philosophy that is now destined to make this a better world in which to live. The greatest achievements of mankind were at first nothing but dreams in the minds of men and women who knew that dreams are the seedlings of all achievements. A burning desire to be and to do is the starting point from which the dreamer must take off. In the science of success philosophy, I have given the means by which this fire of burning desire can be kindled by the humblest person. The world no longer scoffs at the dreamer nor calls him impractical, but instead it beckons to him to bring forth the products of his imagination and sets up before him prizes of both fame and money, the equivalent of a king's ransom.

Commentator:

Dr. Hill, what about the person who has been defeated so often that he has accepted defeat as failure and has given up the hope of personal achievement? Does your philosophy hold any sort of hope for this person?

Dr. Hill:

Well, one of the most encouraging foundations of hope for those who have met with adversity consists in the fact that practically all of the great successes in life began through failure and defeat. Beethoven was deaf, and Milton was blind, yet they enriched the world for ages to come. And Milo C. Jones was stricken by double paralysis before he discovered that he had a brain with which he could make life pay off on his own terms. He put that brain to work, and it yielded the idea of Little Pig Sausage company, which made him a huge fortune. Helen Keller became deaf and blind shortly after birth, yet she conquered all these handicaps and made herself a great source of inspiration to those who are inclined to accept adversity as being failure. The students of the science of success philosophy learn how to reveal the seed of an equivalent benefit that comes with all adversities, and they know how to germinate that seed and develop it into success.

Science of Success

Commentator:

What are some of the personal changes that take place in those who become students of your science of success?

Dr. Hill:

Well, I could write a book in answering that question. First of all, this philosophy helps the student to master all forms of fear and to become a free agent. It also inspires the student to adopt a spirit of self-reliance and removes all inferiority complexes. It develops an alert imagination, and it inspires enthusiasm. It teaches the student to think accurately and relieves him of the costly mistake of snap judgment. It makes the student resourceful so that he quickly finds the answer to all of his problems. It develops a pleasing personality that enables the student to negotiate with other people without opposition, and, of course, it helps one to sell his way through life without friction. It eliminates the costly habit of procrastination and helps one to move with Definiteness of Purpose in everything he does. It teaches the student how to make prayer effective to connect with Infinite Intelligence, and it also helps the student to budget his time so as to make it yield greater returns with less effort.

Commentator:

I get the impression from what you've just said, Dr. Hill, that your science of success philosophy might help any individual to put his religion to a very practical use in connection with the business of making a living in this realistic world.

Dr. Hill:

Yes, I have had many reports from several parts of the country to the effect that the science of success put sound legs under the religion of many of my students, and I have heard some of my students who are in the clergy say that they considered it as applied Christianity.

Commentator:

I think that's wonderful. Thank you, Dr. Hill. Friends, please join us next time as Napoleon Hill further explains the background and foundation of his philosophy of success.

TWO

THE MASTER KEY

Commentator:

You have stated, Dr. Hill, that thinking is the major factor in attaining riches, and perhaps you have heard about the two men talking on this subject. Said the first, "When I was twenty, I made up my mind to get rich." "But," protested the second, "you never did get rich." "No," said the first, "by the time I was twenty-one I decided that it was easier to change my mind."

Dr. Hill:

Well, that is the way too many people go. They want an easy way to riches, you know, but they don't expect to give anything in return for it.

A Sure Way to Riches

Commentator:

What most people want to know right at this point, Dr. Hill, is this: Do you have a sure way to riches?

Dr. Hill:

Yes, indeed I do. If I didn't, I wouldn't be on this program.

Commentator:

Well, good. Now what is it called, how does it work, and how can we all get some of it?

Dr. Hill:

Well, it is called the Master Key to Riches, and it works just as surely and just as scientifically as the law of growth in the vegetable world. Those who possess and use this key may attain all of the riches of this life they can possibly use, but by no other means may riches be attained and retained.

Commentator:

That is an amazing statement, Dr. Hill. It certainly sounds like something that every person should know about. Now will you tell us more?

Dr. Hill:

Well, this Master Key is an ingenious device. It opens the door to sound health, it opens the door to love and romance, it opens the door to enduring friendship by revealing traits of personality and character that make enduring friends. It reveals the method by which every adversity, every failure, every disappointment, every mistaken error of judgment, and every defeat may be transmuted into riches of priceless value. And it rekindles the dead hopes of all who possess it through that state of mind known as faith. It lifts humble men into positions of power, fame, and fortune. It turns back the hands of time and renews the spirit of youth for those who have grown old too soon. It provides the method by which you may take full and complete possession of your own mind, thus giving unchallenged control over the emotions of the heart and the power of thinking. It bridges the deficiencies of inadequate formal schooling and puts one substantially on the same plain of opportunity that is enjoyed by those who have a better education. And lastly, it opens the doors one by one to the twelve great riches of life, which I shall describe for you in detail in these broadcasts. I invite you to listen carefully to what I have to say. Listen not only with open ears but with open minds and eager hearts, remembering that no man will hear that for which he will not listen.

Plural Personality

Commentator:

Well, it sounds like a Master Key to Riches is exactly what I want. Will you give me one so that I can start getting rich?

Dr. Hill:

Well, in order to prepare yourself to use the Master Key to Riches, there are things that you must do.

Commentator:

Well, Dr. Hill, I am willing to put myself in your hands and do exactly as you say so that I may receive all the riches of which you speak.

Dr. Hill:

In order to properly understand the use of the success principles we shall discuss over these broadcasts, it is first necessary to understand something about yourself. It is necessary to evaluate the riches you already possess in order that these other riches may be intelligently added to your life. In order to understand yourself, it is necessary to recognize that every person is a plural personality. You and every other person consist of at least two different personalities. There is of course that self you see when you look in the mirror. That is your physical self, but it is only the house in which your other selves live. In that house are two individuals who are eternally in conflict with each other. One is a negative person who thinks and moves and lives in an atmosphere of doubt, poverty, and ill health. This negative self expects failure and seldom is disappointed. This self thinks of the circumstances of life that you do not want, but which you seem forced to accept: poverty, greed, superstition, fear, doubt, worry, and physical sickness. And one is your other self, a positive person who thinks in terms of opulence, sound health, love and friendship, personal achievement, Creative Vision, and service to others, and who guides you willingly to the attainment of all of these blessings. It is this self alone that is capable of recognizing and appropriating the great riches of life. It is the only self that is capable of receiving the Master Key to Riches.

Commentator:

Well, I am sure that many people are interested in learning more about these imaginary personalities, Dr. Hill.

Dr. Hill:

Let no one be deceived, they are not imaginary personalities of which I speak, they are real and they have been revealed through science and investigations of irreproachable authenticity.

As someone has said, man is wonderfully made, isn't he? Yes, and that is only the beginning. In each person the Creator has constructed a modern radio broadcasting and receiving station so powerful that it picks up and sends out thoughts from or to many parts of the world, and it can even reach out and tune in the power that runs this great universe. Your radio station operates automatically and continuously when you are asleep and when you are awake, and it is under the control at all times of one or the other of your two major personalities—the negative personality or the positive personality.

When the negative personality is in control, your private radio station picks up only the negative thoughts, which are being sent out by hundreds of millions of other negative personalities throughout the world. Now, these are accepted, acted upon, and translated into their physical equivalent in terms of the circumstances of life that you do not want.

When your positive personality is in control, it picks up only the positive thoughts being released by millions of other positive personalities throughout the world and transmits them into their physical equivalents in terms of prosperity and the things you do want: sound health, love, hope, faith, peace of mind, and happiness—the values of life for which you and every other person are searching.

The Richest Man on the Face of the Earth

Commentator:

Well, that is quite inspiring. You have mentioned our positive self and our negative self, Dr. Hill. Is it so important to keep a positive mental attitude?

Dr. Hill:

The richest man on the face of the earth is a man with a positive mental attitude.

Commentator:

You have stopped me in my tracks, Dr. Hill. I thought we were going to discuss money on this program. Isn't this program called "Think and Grow Rich"?

Dr. Hill:

Yes, it is, and there is the key to riches. If we are to be rich, if we are to attain positive things in this world, we have to start with a positive mental attitude. What sort of riches do you think can be attained if you go around with a sour, melancholy, negative attitude all the time? Can you tell me how a negative attitude can create anything good?

Commentator:

I don't believe I can, but a lot of people seem to try it just the same. I know a lot of people who try to get things done by being sour. I know of many people who try to force their way through life by fighting it. Now, don't they attain some measure of riches?

Dr. Hill:

Perhaps they do, but whatever they gain is more than offset by their lack of enjoyment of it. Their negative mental attitude reduces their enjoyment of the things they possess down to near absolute zero.

Commentator:

I won't tell you how old I was before I really came to know that statement is true. I thought people who possessed money were happy because they possessed money.

Dr. Hill:

Now, don't you believe a word of it. The fact that some people have money may be just the reason why they are not happy. They have just one of the riches of life, and it takes more of them to enjoy life completely. On these radio programs I shall reveal the secret of the great Master Key to Riches to as many of you as are prepared to receive it, but let me warn you that this Master Key may be retained only by those who accept the obligation to share it with others. No man may use it selfishly and hope to retain the Master Key for any length of time.

I shall reveal to you the means by which you may share the blessings of the Master Key, but the responsibility of sharing must be your own. I am speaking of material riches, of course, but I am not speaking of material riches alone. It is my hope and my purpose to share with you the knowledge by which you may acquire all riches through the expression of your own personal initiative. So, on these radio programs I shall assume that you wish to become very rich in financial and nonfinancial respects, and I invite you to become partners with me in the attainment of your desire, because I have found a way to attain all riches and I am prepared to serve as your guide. For years I followed the path to riches the hard way, before I learned that there is a short and dependable path that I could have followed had I been guided as I hope to guide you.

Enduring Riches

Commentator:

Dr. Hill, since we have been talking about riches, I have been wondering if I really know what riches are. You say money is not necessarily riches. How can the average person tell when he has riches; maybe we already have riches and do not recognize them. Just what are riches, anyway?

Dr. Hill:

That is an excellent point, so let us clear it up immediately. Enduring riches consist of many values other than material things, and may I add that without these other intangible values, the possession of money cannot possibly bring the happiness that some people think it will provide. Whenever I think of riches, I have in mind the greater riches whose possessors have made life pay off on their own terms, the terms of true and complete happiness. I call these "the great riches of life," and it is my sincere desire to share them with all of you who will prepare yourselves to receive them. You may wonder about my willingness to share. Let me tell you that the Master Key to Riches enables its possessors to add to their own store of riches everything of value that they share with others. This is one of the strangest facts of life, but it is a fact that each one of you must recognize and respect if you hope to become really, really rich in this world.

Commentator:

Did I hear you correctly, sir? Did I understand you to intimate that one must share his riches with others, or they are not riches?

Dr. Hill:

Yes, sir, you heard me correctly.

Commentator:

Well, do you mean that I can't be rich by myself, that I couldn't enjoy a million dollars all by myself if someone gave it to me?

Dr. Hill:

Believe me when I tell you that it cannot be done. The human being is constructed so that everything that happens to him happens in his mind, and he must have company, in misery or in joy, in riches or in success. A person was not made to live alone. So you can no more be rich or successful entirely alone than you can fly. On a later program I shall show you why no man ever became a success alone.

Let us remember also that a state of mind is the one and only thing over which any person has complete, unchallenged right of control. It is highly significant that the Creator created man with control over nothing except the power to shape his own thoughts and the privilege of fitting them to any pattern. Mental attitude is important because it converts the brain to the equivalent of the electromagnet, which attracts one's dominating thoughts, aims, and purposes. If your thoughts are positive, they are most certainly attractive, and they will attract things of a positive and beneficial nature. If they are negative, you may be sure you will attract the counterpart: fears, worries, and doubts. With your thinking you will write your own ticket to success or to failure.

A Positive Mental Attitude

Commentator:

The tremendous popularity of your book *Think and Grow Rich* proves to me that men and women everywhere are anxious to learn more of your rules for success. So would you start at the beginning and tell us what kind of attitude will put us on the road to riches and how we may prepare ourselves to become rich?

Dr. Hill:

A positive mental attitude is the first of the great riches, the starting point of all riches, whether they be riches of a material nature or an intangible nature. It attracts the riches of true friendship and the riches one finds in the hope of future achievement. It also provides the riches one will find in nature's handiwork as it exists in the moonlit night, in the stars that float out there in the heavens, in the exquisite landscapes, in distant horizons, and the riches to be found in the labor of love of one's own choice where expression may be given to the highest goals of one's own soul.

It provides the riches of harmony in our relationships where all members of the family work together in the spirit of friendly cooperation. It provides the riches of sound physical health, which is the treasure of those who have learned to balance work with play and worship with rest, and who have learned the wisdom of eating to live rather than living to eat. It provides the riches of freedom from fear and the riches of enthusiasm and the riches of song and laughter and the riches of self-discipline, as to which one will have the joy of knowing that the mind can and will serve any desired end if one will take possession and command it with a Definiteness of Purpose.

A positive mental attitude provides the riches of play where one may lay aside all of the burdens of life and become like a little child; the riches of discovery of one's other self, that self that knows no such reality as permanent failure; the riches of faith in the Infinite Intelligence of which every individual is a minute part; and the riches of meditation, the connecting bridge by which one may draw upon the great universal supply of the Infinite Intelligence at will. Yes, these and all other riches begin with a positive mental attitude, so it is easy to see that this is without question the greatest of all the great riches of life.

Andrew Carnegie's Formula

Commentator:

Would you care to give your listeners a hint as to the nature of the Andrew Carnegie formula for success, which you have referred to as the Master Key to Riches?

Dr. Hill:

Well, the Master Key consists of the seventeen success principles I organized from the lifetime experiences of more than five hundred of the top-ranking businessmen of America, among them Henry Ford, Thomas A. Edison, Dr. Alexander Graham Bell, and Andrew Carnegie. The first and most important of these seventeen success principles is a definite major purpose. No one can rise above mediocrity without a definite objective and a definite plan for attaining it. The truly great successes are attained only by those who adopt a major definite purpose.

Commentator:

Dr. Hill, do you mean that the person who reaches a higher bracket of success must have one particular aim in life that stands out over and above all his minor desires?

Dr. Hill:

Yes, sir, that is correct. In my writings I have described the precise method one must follow in order to attain the object of his definite major purpose in life. And you may be interested in knowing that this famous success formula is believed to have made fortunes for more people than any other influence in the history of civilization.

Commentator:

Thank you, Dr. Napoleon Hill. Your explanation has helped us to clearly evaluate the riches that come from a positive mental attitude. Your radio audience will want to know more about your philosophy that enables people to think and grow rich. Everyone is invited to tune in to these upcoming broadcasts.

Dr. Hill:

In our broadcasts in this series, I will concentrate on a full explanation of what I consider to be the Big Five of the seventeen success principles: Definiteness of Purpose, the Mastermind, Applied Faith, Going the Extra Mile, and Creative Vision. I consider these principles to be the most important, the five essential Foundations for Success. Before we discuss the Big Five, however, our next broadcast will explain the important role of self-discipline in learning and applying these principles.

THREE

THE DEPARTMENTS OF THE MIND

Dr. Hill:

Someone has said that if you gain control over yourself, you may have control over everything else within the sphere of space you occupy in the world, and I think that is substantially true. This control is accomplished by self-discipline, which is necessary to apply the Big Five success principles.

The Fourteen Major Emotions

Self-discipline starts by gaining control over the fourteen major emotions, seven of which are positive and seven of which are negative. There are seven other factors that must be under control, and they constitute all there is of the departments of the mind with which we think.

These seven departments of the mind are as follows:

1. The Ego is the Seat of Willpower (You must get control over the ego, so that you can lift it up or deflate it according to where you want it to be.)
2. The Faculty of the Emotions
3. The Faculty of Reason

4. The Faculty of the Imagination
5. The Faculty of the Conscience
6. The Faculty of Memory
7. The Five Senses

These are the only factors, the only departments with which you carry on the business of thinking, and if you truly and really have discipline, you will have all of them under control.

The seven positive emotions, by the way, are not all of the emotions, but they are the seven emotions of greatest importance:

1. Love
2. Sex
3. Hope
4. Faith
5. Enthusiasm
6. Loyalty
7. Desire

The seven negative emotions, which also must be under control, are:

1. Fear
2. Jealousy
3. Hatred
4. Revenge
5. Greed
6. Anger
7. Superstition

Speaking for a moment on the subject of anger, you hear people say every day how they became so angry at someone for what they said or did. Now, no one can make you angry without your cooperation—you have to cooperate. I defy you to make me angry unless I want to become angry. Of course, I might do it on my own account without your help, too. But I certainly am not going to let you boil me over and cause me to lose my head and do some unsound thinking and say something I will regret. If I am using my head properly, and if I have the right amount of discipline, I will never let that occur.

I can remember a time when people did make me angry, and I responded in order to let them know exactly what was going on. You know, that is an old trick some people use to find out what is in your mind. They will make you angry, and when you are in a state of anger, you are not quite yourself, and you open your mouth and let words fly out that you wish you had kept in.

The four big musts that need to be under control at all times to maintain self-discipline are:

1. The Appetite for Food and Drink
2. The Mental Attitude
3. The Budgeting of Time
4. Definiteness of Purpose

"Auto-suggestion" is a suggestion you make to yourself and is the medium by which self-discipline becomes a habit, and the starting point in the development of self-discipline is Definiteness of Purpose. Obsessional desire is the dynamo that gives life and action to Definiteness of Purpose. Be careful what you set your heart upon—your obsessional desire—because the subconscious mind goes to work translating that desire into a material equivalent.

Self-discipline cannot be attained overnight; it must be developed step by step, by the formation of definite habits of thought and action. It is surprising what you can do with your mind if you take possession of it and use it the way the Creator intended you should use it, and that is to project your mind to the object of the things you want most in life and to keep your mind fixed upon that and not on the things you don't want.

Dr. Hill's Ten Rules

I am going to give you ten rules for obtaining and maintaining profitable self-discipline. These are rules of my own making; some of them are very simple, but they will be very helpful.

One is to keep cool when other people get hot. I know you can agree with that one, but I am not so sure you will always live up to it. We are inclined, all of us, to get hot when the other person gets hot, and to say angry things when the other person starts saying angry things.

I was in the home of the president of a big electric power company one evening when there came a storm, and he called up one of his headmen to go and take care of an emergency that was a result of that storm. It was a Sunday evening. The man was gone about two hours, and when he returned, he came up on the front porch of the home of the company president and called him out on the porch, and I never heard a man get such a tongue-lashing in all my life as this president of the electric power company got. The worker said, "You called on me because you are the president of the company, and I can solve problems, and I am just as good as you are." Oh, his tirade was terrific.

I heard only one side of the conversation because there was only one side to it. One man was doing all the talking, and one man was doing all the listening. And after this had been going on for three minutes, the other man ran out of wind and had nothing more to say; he was mad, you see, because they had called him out on this stormy night. I heard the president close the door, and he came back and just smiled and said, "Why, the man was a little bit hot, wasn't he?" That is all he said—"a little bit hot, wasn't he?"

I had expected to hear fists begin to fly out there at any moment, but you see here was a man who had risen to great heights of achievement financially and had done it by self-discipline, and he didn't propose to allow that workman, who had been temporarily unbalanced by his anger, to throw him off-balance and make him stoop to his level.

You will notice when you get into an argument with anyone—and you are apt to if you don't watch yourself—but if you just remain silent while the other fellow is blowing off his top, he finally gets to the point where he has no more top to blow off. Then, if you want to get in a few words of your own, that is a mighty good place to do it. It is a fine thing if the words you get in aren't the kind of words you have been hearing. Say something kind in return. It is far better for the other person and far better for you. It shows you to be the bigger of the two of you. Anybody can get mad and blow his top because of what somebody does or says, and it happens all the time. But the truly big person who is in charge of himself doesn't allow anybody to draw him down to the level of a street brawl or an argument in harsh words.

Number two in my rules of self-discipline: remember, there are three sides to all arguments. We ordinarily think there are two sides to an argument, but there are not—there are three. There is your side, there is the other person's side, and then there is the right side, which is usually about in the middle of the two points. Remember that when you get into an argument with the other person. Don't assume he is always at fault; maybe you are partly at fault, too. Maybe neither of you is totally at fault. The chances are in all arguments I have ever heard that both parties were partly to blame in one way or another.

Number three: never give directives to a subordinate when you are angry. If the matter is urgent, then cool off quickly before giving orders.

Number four: treat all people as if they were rich relatives from whom you expect to inherit something after their death. Now, that's a good one, that's a honey, if you just do that. If you had a rich relative who had a million dollars he was going to leave to you, or you suspected that he was going to, it wouldn't make very much difference what he said or did. He would never throw you off-balance. You would never talk back to him, would you? Of course you wouldn't. You would be quite silly if you did. Keeping quiet for a million dollars seems to me to be a very nice, easy price to pay.

Number five: look for the seed of an equivalent benefit in every unpleasant circumstance you meet, no matter what the unpleasant circumstance is. Don't wait a week or two till you work yourself up about it. Start right in where you stand; it will lessen the blow. It will lessen the hurt of the wound, whatever it happens to be, if you start looking for that seed of equivalent benefit.

Number six: learn the almost forgotten art of asking questions and listening to the answers, instead of getting the other person told off. It gives you an awful lot of satisfaction when you are angry to get the other person told off, doesn't it? The temptation is very great to do that. I know because I have been there many times. Don't do it. Be bigger than that. Listen to what the other person has to say, and then, when somebody makes a statement you are not sure about, learn to ask this one question. It is one of the most important questions in life. It will serve more purposes than any other short question I can think of. When somebody makes a statement that you are not sure about, or that you doubt, or that you question, ask a four-word question: "How do you know?" Then wait for an answer and see them back up. Instead of getting into an argument and making an incident of the matter and getting yourself worked up into an argument, let the other person stew in his own fat by putting him over a barrel with that question: "How do you know?"

I had a clergyman in my class who was very—well, I don't know just exactly how to describe it. He was a fanatic, you might say, on the subject of religion, and he was sure that he knew what was going to happen to me after death. He said so in no uncertain terms, not in the class, but in a private conversation. He raved and ranted for quite a little while about it, and when he got through, I said, "Well, how do you know, Parson?" That really put him over a barrel. He said, "Well, that is the way I feel about it; that is my faith." I said, "Well now, having belief and faith is one thing, and having evidence is something else. How do you know what is going to happen to me after I die? I don't know, and I doubt that you do. How do you know?" He never gave a satisfactory answer.

Number seven of my rules for obtaining self-discipline: never say or do anything that may influence another person without first asking yourself, "Will it benefit him or hurt him?" And if it will hurt him, don't do it. Don't say anything or do anything that will hurt another person under any circumstances, no matter how much he may deserve it. Exercise self-discipline. If you hurt another person, you are going to hurt yourself ten times as much at least, because that hurt will come back on you. I don't care who you are or what circumstances you are working under or living under. If you hurt another person, you will be hurt ten times as much, and if the hurt doesn't come immediately, the rate of interest on that, compound interest upon compound interest, will be a hundred times as great if you wait long enough. Because everything you do to or for another person, you do to or for yourself. There is no escape from that.

That is just as much a law as the law of gravitation, which everyone understands. You know that if you stepped off the top of a building, no matter what your frame of mind was or what your belief happened to be, the law of gravitation would apply, and you would hit the ground and die in a very few seconds. This law that brings you back what you send out is just as inevitable and just as sound as the law of gravitation or any other of nature's laws.

Number eight: learn the difference between friendly analysis and unfriendly criticism; then decide which you wish to live by in your relations with others. Now, friendly analysis is one thing and is welcomed by most sensible people. I don't object to friendly analysis of anything that I do, even if it is very unfavorable; if it is friendly analysis, I like it because I can improve on it. But if it is unfriendly criticism, then I resent it. I wouldn't be human if I didn't.

How can I tell whether it is friendly analysis or unfriendly criticism? How would you go about telling? There are a lot of ways you can tell. You can tell by your relationship to the person who is making it whether it is friendly or unfriendly to begin with. If it is an enemy, obviously I would discount it right off the bat because you almost know that it is going to be unfriendly criticism. I can tell also by the tone of voice in which he does it, by the manner in which he does it, because someone who engages in unfriendly criticism generally uses a few epithets along with it that clearly indicate he is biased. If you have self-discipline, you are not going to be influenced by that kind of a person.

Number nine: remember that a good leader in any calling is one who can take orders as cheerfully as he can give them.

Number ten: last but not the least, remember that tolerance in human relations is just as important as any other rule of self-discipline.

The Hatfields and the McCoys

I want to give you some examples of what a lack of self-discipline can do. I come from down in Virginia, and our adjoining sister state is West Virginia, where my sons now live, and we know the Hatfields and the McCoys on both sides. We have known them back down through the years. Several generations ago all the Hatfields' pigs got into the McCoys' cornfields, and a McCoy set his dog on a pig and it tore his ear off. The pig wasn't worth more than a dollar and a half at the most, but they started shooting one another on sight over that pig, and I don't know how many Hatfields and how many McCoys have been killed, but it has been quite a number.

Now, somewhere along the way somebody failed to use self-discipline. That feud became famous all over the country. If any one of you hasn't heard about the Hatfields and McCoys, I'd be surprised. It wasn't an imaginary feud; it was a real one.

The habit of making an incident out of petty annoyances is one of the things that most of us indulge in very greatly almost every day of our lives, instead of just looking at them, or winking at them, or keeping silent.

The man who exercises self-discipline doesn't allow anybody else to make an incident that he doesn't want to occur. Life, even if it is filled with unpleasant things one must deal with, need not fan the fire of an unpleasant incident into the white heat of the argument. You can always avoid it if you try. You say, "Oh, but my pride." The heck with your pride!

Most cases of pride are just stubbornness. Forget about your pride; you don't have to listen to everything you hear, if it is insulting. Of course, you don't have to let someone hit you on both sides of the cheek, either, before you knock his teeth down his throat, but at least let him have one chance at you before you start doing that.

You know, a very small incident can make a feud just like the Hatfield-McCoy feud that lasted down through the years, and it destroys your appetite and gives you stomach ulcers, gives you headaches, causes your teeth to decay sooner than they would otherwise, and the Lord only knows what else it does to you. Why let an insignificant incident annoy you and disturb you, throw you off-balance? Don't do it. Be more dignified than that, be more becoming, be more appreciative of the great prerogative the Creator gave you; that is, the ability to control your own mind and make it whatever you want it to be.

Never try to settle an incident by force, strong language, or coercion. Properly timed salesmanship can do a better job. Petty conversation and gossip often lead to unpleasant incidents. If you can't find something pleasant to talk about, it would be better for you if you just listened. I suppose the greatest compliment I have ever had was paid to me by the late Dr. William Plumer Jacobs, the president of Presbyterian

College in Clinton, South Carolina, with whom I was associated for two years. After I had been there a whole year, and after we had had many business discussions and personal and social conversations about politics and religion and everything else, he turned to me one day and said, "You know the thing I like best about you?"

I said, "No, I don't. What is it?"

He said, "You never engage in any petty conversation."

I didn't. And if anybody else started those conversations, I either remained silent or got up and made it my business to have a walk around the block. The mental attitude by which you relate yourself to incidents represents the crossroads of your life, at which you take the grand boulevard to success or the rocky road to failure.

Applying Self-Discipline

Now, I want to give you some idea as to the points in which self-discipline should be applied; and I am sure that somewhere along the line, if you are checking yourself against each of these suggestions, you will find some benefits. Most people are failures all through their lives because they lack self-discipline, and here are some of the vital circumstances in connection with which failure in self-discipline leads to failure in other things as well. Here is where self-discipline must begin.

First, in failure to adopt and live by a definite purpose and a definite plan. You need self-discipline in connection with that, because if you don't have it, you are not going to adopt that definite purpose and that definite plan; or if you do adopt it, you are going to neglect it and not carry it out.

Second, you are going to need self-discipline to refrain from accepting from life anything you don't want, and I do mean anything and everything. I have never in my whole life accepted anything from life that I didn't want. I can truthfully say to you today in all sincerity, if I have anything on the face of the earth that I can use, or need, or want, or desire, I have it in abundance, and I got it by keeping my mind fixed upon the things I want and off the things I don't want.

Next, you need self-discipline in taking possession of your mind, which is the one thing nature intended that you should do. Make it a habit. Make it a series of habits. Take possession of your own mind, and do not allow the circumstances of life or other peoples' words, or other peoples' thoughts, or other peoples' beliefs, or anything else, to deprive you of the privilege of making your mind whatever you want it to be. That is the greatest form of self-discipline in which you can possibly engage, because that is the thing that will make you a self-determining, free, independent individual, and nothing else will.

Next, end the habit of limiting yourself to insufficient self-confidence. In the final analysis there is only one great person in the world. You are the greatest person in the world from your own inner viewpoint. You sell yourself short if you discount yourself so as to not believe in yourself. You are not exercising self-discipline in the way that nature intended you should.

Next, end the habit of allowing the mind to think more often of failure than it does of success and thus developing failure consciousness. People who succeed keep their minds fixed upon the success side of life, and they develop, thereby, success consciousness, and that consciousness begins to operate automatically and attracts to them opportunities. It attracts to them people who want to cooperate. You take any successful man, and I want to tell you that everything he touches turns into gold. You take a man who is a failure, and everything he touches turns to dust or something less than dust because he has a failure consciousness. And as sure as you are sitting in this room tonight, the affairs, the things that happen to you, the things that you attract to you correspond to your state of mind, and you control that state of mind. Just make it anything you wish it to be, and that is self-discipline in its highest form.

In my next broadcasts I will explore with you the Big Five Principles of Success and tell you how you must use self-discipline to attain and maintain them.

FOUR
ONE'S GREATEST PURPOSE

Dr. Hill:

Welcome, friends. Tonight, I will discuss Definiteness of Purpose, the first of the Big Five Principles of Success.

The Seven Factors

There are seven factors that enter into this subject of Definiteness of Purpose. I am going to give you an outline of the seven. They constitute the warp and woof of this principle and give you the reason why it is the beginning of all success, because psychological, economic, and philosophical factors of a definite major purpose consist entirely in these seven premises. The first premise or factor follows.

Purpose, Plan, and Action

The starting point of all achievements is the adoption of a definite purpose accompanied by a definite plan for its attainment, followed by an appropriate action. That means purpose, plan, and action; those three words constitute the first factor.

Now, there has never been known to be success in any calling except as a result of Definiteness of Purpose. We all have purposes, varying purposes, but they aren't definite; most often they are hopes and wishes. We all wish for money, we wish for opportunity, we wish for love and affection, we wish for recognition, we wish for a lot of things, but wishing is not quite enough. Before you can be sure of success, you have to have a definite objective, a definite plan for getting it, and you have to back that plan with everything you have. You have to use your mind constantly until the subconscious section of the mind picks up your plan and finds out what it is that you want.

Motives and Fears

The second premise is that all individual achievements are the result of a motive or a combination of motives. You have never heard of anybody accomplishing anything in this world, or doing anything in this world, except as a result of a motive. All people move as a result of motives, and there are nine basic motives under which you can classify every impulse that you have to do or not do things throughout life. Here they are.

Number one is the emotion of love. Number two is the emotion of sex. Number three is the emotion for material wealth. These are known as the Big Three, and it has been said that these three emotions practically govern the entire world, and I don't think that is an overstatement by any means.

Number four is the desire for self-preservation, and number five is the desire for freedom of body and mind. Number six is the desire for personal expression and recognition; that is an outstanding motive. Number seven is the desire for perpetuation of life after death. Those are the seven positives. Now, here come the two negative motives that influence your lives very often more than the positives, and these are the ones you have to look out for. Number eight is the desire for revenge, and you would be surprised how much of one's life is devoted to wanting to strike back at somebody for some imaginary or real grievance, and yet all such effort is destructive. Number nine is the grandfather of them all. Guess what that is? It probably influences more human action than all other motives combined. And yet it is the most destructive of them all. Number nine is the emotion of fear, and under that heading there are six basic fears, six things that you have to be on the lookout for constantly all the way through life.

Number one is the fear of poverty. Now, why anyone should be afraid of poverty in a great nation like this, where opportunity abounds on every hand, is more than I can understand. But I do know that the vast majority of my students have to be treated first for the fear of poverty; they have to be made success-conscious. You will never be successful in anything until you become success-conscious. You have to get over the idea of self-limitation. The second of the six basic fears is the fear of criticism, and you are lucky indeed if you have come this far in life, all of you or any of you, without having suffered the fear of criticism, the fear of what "they" will say. And I have heard so many people say, "Well, I would do so-and-so if it weren't for what 'they' would say," and I have never yet found out who "they" are. They are entirely imaginary human beings, but you would be surprised how powerful they are. They stupefy enthusiasm, they cut down your personal initiative, they destroy your imagination, and they make it practically impossible for you to accomplish anything above mediocrity.

Number three is the fear of ill health. Doctors know all too well what that fear does. It results in a condition known as hypochondria or imaginary illness.

Number four is the fear of a loss of love from someone, upon which that form of schizophrenia known as jealousy is based. Jealousy doesn't require a reason; it can be just as violent and just as destructive where there is no basis for it, as where there is a basis. But it is a motivating force and a fear.

Number five is the fear of old age. I don't know why men and women should be afraid that they are going to dry up and blow away when they get to that nice ripe old age of forty to fifty. The real achievements of the world were the result of men and women who had gone well beyond the age of fifty, and the greatest age of achievement was between sixty-five and seventy-five, so I don't know why one should be afraid of old age, but nevertheless people are.

And the last one, the grandfather of them all, is the fear of death. It's the rarest thing in the world to find a person who hasn't at some time or other been afraid of dying. Before you finish listening to these broadcasts, I hope we will prepare you to eliminate all of these basic fears, particularly the last one.

A Burning Desire

The third premise of Definiteness of Purpose is that any dominating idea, plan, or purpose held in the mind through repetition of thought and which is emotionalized with a burning desire for its realization is taken over by the subconscious section of the mind and acted upon through whatever natural and logical means may be available. In the slang of the day, there is a mouthful in that sentence.

The key ideas in that sentence are "natural and logical means" and "a burning desire." A burning desire is one you take to bed with you at night. You give it over to your subconscious mind at night, and you get up with it in the morning. You eat with it, you sleep with it, you first get it and then it gets you; now that is what a burning desire is. You may have to talk about it, you may have to think about it; however, when it comes to talking about it, be careful where you talk because you may become boresome to somebody. Some of the things I am going to tell you about may seem fantastic; some of them you may never have done before. Just don't take a part of this philosophy, take it exactly as I give it to you, and no matter how foolish it may seem to you or to those around you at the beginning, follow it to the letter.

The fourth premise is that any dominating desire, plan, or purpose backed by that state of mind known as faith is taken over by the subconscious section of the mind and acted upon almost immediately.

The Power of Thought

The fifth premise, the power of thought, is the only thing over which any human being has complete, unquestionable control. The fact is so astounding that it connotes a close relationship between the mind of man and his Infinite Intelligence. The very fact that the Creator gave humans control over only one thing is because it was intended that one thing should be sufficient for people's needs, and believe you me it is sufficient if you use it properly.

There isn't anything you can't achieve that you can conceive and believe. If you can conceive an idea or plan or purpose, and you believe that you can achieve it, you can find out ways and means of doing it, but you have to be definite about it, you have to be specific, you have to know why you want it, and you have to make up your mind what you are going to give in return for it, because nature frowns upon the idea of something for nothing.

And the sixth premise, the role of the subconscious section of the mind, appears to be the only doorway of approach to Infinite Intelligence. The basis of the approach is faith based upon Definiteness of Purpose. Any idea, plan, or purpose brought into the mind in the spirit of faith begins almost immediately to reveal to you the ways and means of carrying out that idea.

The seventh premise is that every brain is both a broadcasting set and receiving station for the vibrations of thought. This fact explains the importance of moving with Definiteness of Purpose instead of drifting, since the brain may be so thoroughly charged with the nature of one's purpose that it will begin to attract a physical or material equivalent of that purpose. That is an astounding thing, ladies and gentlemen, all the more so because it is a provable fact that the first broadcasting and receiving set ever built was the brain of man, and, whether you recognize it or not, you are constantly tuning in to the vibrations of other people, especially the other people with whom you are in harmony—I mean where your thoughts and their thoughts agree. If your thoughts happen to be of poverty, of failure, or of illness, why, you tune in to the thoughts of all other people who are releasing similar thoughts. If your thoughts are dominated by thoughts of success and riches, opulence, you will tune in to the thoughts of other people who think along those lines.

Bring Me the Winner

There will be times when ideas will flash into your mind that are so negative they almost scare you. You wonder where they came from, you wonder why your mind would hand over such destructive thoughts, and if the truth were known, you left your receiving set open and tuned in to the wrong type of mind. This philosophy is designed to keep your receiving set closed to all except the kind of minds you want, and those are positive minds, minds that think in terms of what you want instead of what you don't want. I think one of the strangest things in life is that most people go all the way through life—regardless of their education, their standing, or their opportunity—as failures.

They suffer with fears and limitations, and, strictly speaking, they never find happiness. The reason, if you examine it, is that they allow their minds to dwell upon failure, poverty, ill health, and the things they don't want. The mind has a peculiar way of attracting to you the things it feeds upon, things it associates with. A failure is like a rotten apple in a barrel, and you can't afford to have it, you can't afford close association with people who are not vibrating on all twelve cylinders. Pick out the winners, be like the man who went to a restaurant and ordered the lobster, and when they brought it out one of its big claws was gone. He complained about it, and the waiter said, "Well, he got in a fight and lost that one." "Well," the customer said, "bring me the winner. I want the winner." Now, that is the idea exactly: associate with winners because they will do something for you, and if you associate with failures, they will do something to you in spite of all you do.

The Benefits

Here are the benefits that come out of a major purpose. First of all, Definiteness of Purpose automatically develops self-reliance; it develops personal initiative, imagination, enthusiasm, self-discipline, and concentration of effort—all of these being prerequisites for success and of vital importance. That is just one of the things that Definiteness of Purpose does.

Number two, it induces one to budget one's time and to plan day-to-day endeavors that lead to attainment of one's major purpose. If you have really got a definite major purpose, as distinguished from the many minor purposes you may have, you will find that never a day goes by but what some opportunity is available to you, whereby you can advance yourself toward that purpose. It may be only one step, but you'll certainly find that opportunity.

Number three, a definite purpose makes one more alert in recognizing opportunities related to the object of that purpose and inspires the courage to embrace and act upon those opportunities.

Number four, Definiteness of Purpose inspires confidence in one's integrity and character and attracts the favorable attention of other people. Did you ever walk down the street in a crowded section of the city where everybody was in from other places and notice how people were inclined to step all over those who didn't know where they were going? Did you ever start through a crowd when you had to make a train, and you just had to get through that crowd, and that is all there was to it, and you were so determined that people looked back over their shoulder and saw you coming and they made sure that they got out of the way to make room for you? That only goes to show that where someone is determined and people see that determination, they get out of his way and cooperate. You can test it anywhere you please, and you will find it works out that way.

Number five, perhaps the greatest of all the benefits of a definite purpose, is that it opens the way for the full exercise of that state of mind known as faith, by making the mind positive and freeing it from limitations of fear, doubt, discouragement, indecision, and procrastination.

The sixth and last major benefit of Definiteness of Purpose is that it makes one success-conscious; that is to say your mind thinks in terms of success. You never think about the no-can-do; you think about the can-do of everything you tackle. The only difference between Henry Ford and tens of thousands of men who worked for him was the fact that he could place his mind on the can-do part of any problem, and most of the others placed their mind on the no-can-do—they could see the hole but not the doughnut. That was the distinguishing thing of all else that made Henry Ford the great industrialist he was. He had great capacity to focus his mind upon that part of any circumstance he could handle and keep it off the parts he couldn't handle.

I've noticed that all successful men think that way. You take the average person with problems, give him an opportunity, and what happens? Why, the first thing that happens is he begins to think of all the things prohibiting him from accepting that opportunity, why that problem is going to embarrass him, why he can't solve it. That is not the way a successful mind works.

You give a successful man's mind a problem, and the first thing he does is begin to take it apart. Well, I can handle this, I can handle that, I can handle anything. Maybe there are things I can't handle, but I can handle these and go to work handling them, and by the time I get those handled, why, the others often dissolve and go away. They're not there anymore.

The Instructions

Here are instructions for applying the principle of definite major purpose. First of all write out a clear statement of your major purpose, sign it, commit it to memory, and repeat it orally at least once a day in the form of a prayer or affirmation. That is going to do something that is very obvious to you. It is going to place the full weight of your religion behind you if you believe in a religion, if you are associated with any religion or any religious organization. You use your own religion and place it behind your definite major purpose in the form of prayer. Place all your faith in your Creator; that is step number one. Now, that happens at least once a day, and it may happen fifty times a day—the more the better. The more you repeat this definite major purpose, the more quickly the subconscious mind will take it over and begin to act on it.

The subconscious mind is something like a camera. If you have had any experience at all with a camera, you know that before you can get a clear picture, there are three things that you must do. First of all, you must have the camera focused on the object so as to bring it into clear outline. Second, you must have the right kind of lighting on the object. And third, you must have the right kind of timing. You certainly have to have the same thing in connection with the conveying of pictures to your subconscious mind. If you are not definite, your subconscious mind cannot pick up anything more definite than what is in your mind. You will be surprised oftentimes how you think you've had a definite major purpose, but it has been so indefinite, unfocused, and ill timed that your subconscious didn't act upon it or wouldn't trust it because of its indefiniteness.

Second, write out a clear, definite outline of the plan or plans by which you intend to achieve the object of your purpose: state the maximum amount of time in which you intend to attain it, and describe in detail precisely what you intend to give in return for the realization of your major purpose. Make your plan flexible enough to permit changes anytime you are inspired to do so, remembering that Infinite

Intelligence may present you a better plan than yours. You will find, no doubt, that when you lay out your plan, start to attain the object of your definite major purpose, and find it doesn't work—you put everything you've got behind it, and if that doesn't work, it doesn't mean your purpose isn't right. You don't have to change your purpose; what you need to do is change your plan. Maybe you need to bring into your plan help through the Mastermind principle; that is to say, you need the influence and cooperation of somebody else. Maybe you alone have not been strong enough to put your plan over.

Keep your major purpose strictly to yourself. The reason for this secrecy is that disclosure of your purpose would only serve to give those who are not in sympathy with it an opportunity to defeat you. How would people go about defeating you? Have you ever had the experience of aiming at something far greater than anything you had ever achieved before and made the mistake of telling your relatives about it? Chances are that your relatives are the ones you have to watch the closest, unless you happen to have someone in that group who is very sympathetic with you.

Call your major purpose into your conscious mind as often as may be practical. Eat with it, sleep with it, drink with it, and take it with you wherever you go. Now, by calling it into your conscious mind and visualizing it and seeing yourself already in possession of it, you thereby give your subconscious mind a clear picture of what it is you want. Nobody knows exactly what the subconscious mind is, how it works, or why it works. I don't pretend to know, but I do know that certain buttons you press get results in your subconscious. I can describe to you what to do, and if you do precisely that, you are bound to get results. What it is that brings you results is your guess just as well as mine. I don't know. It might even happen within a matter of minutes after you have started the plan, it might be hours, it might be days, it might be weeks, or it might even be years, depending upon the faith that you put behind it and the intensity with which you want it.

Do you remember Émile Coué, the Frenchman who came over here in about 1920, with his famous formula "every day, in every way, I'm getting better and better"? There were millions of people repeating that phrase, and some of them were getting results, but most of them weren't. Why do you suppose those who didn't get results didn't get them? I will tell you precisely why they didn't. The person who said "day by day I am getting better and better" and believed it got results, and to the fellow who just quoted the words, nothing at all happened, just like in most prayers.

You know, of course, that the vast majority of prayers have only negative results, and if you understand this principle of Definiteness of Purpose, you will understand why prayer doesn't work when you want it to work. The reason being is, generally speaking, when most people go to prayer, they do so only in the time of stress and emergency and when their minds are filled with fear. Their subconscious mind carries out the dominating tendency of the mental attitude, whether it is of faith or of fear. Also, when most people go to prayer, they do not see themselves already in possession of that for which they pray. They hope that it will take place, but they are not sure about it. Consequently, nothing happens but a negative result.

You would be perfectly astounded at how much difference there will be in your prayers after you learn to pray with Definiteness of Purpose and with such enduring faith that you see yourself in possession of the thing you pray for even before you start praying. Your subconscious mind doesn't understand the difference between good and bad. It doesn't understand the difference between success and failure. It will believe anything you tell it, and that being true, why not start telling it of sure success, start telling it that you already have the things you want, and let it know what those things are.

I will give you one illustration that will show you that this is the way the subconscious mind works. You take a person who tells a lie, a little white lie, let us say, not meaning to harm anybody by it, but he tells it over and over again, and finally he gets to the point where he believes it—he doesn't know the difference! After you repeat it often enough to the subconscious mind, you will accept it and act upon it as if it were true.

Now then, as to what one's major purpose in life should be. First of all, it should represent one's greatest purpose in life, the single purpose that above all others a person desires to achieve and the fruits of which one is willing to leave behind him as a monument to himself. That would represent your definite major purpose. I very often have students come to me and say, "Well, Dr. Hill, I have thought about this a lot, and I don't know what it is in life that I want." Ladies and gentlemen, I am helpless with that kind of a student. What one wants in life is every individual's prerogative. It is up to the individual to determine, and I can't do that for anybody. You have got to determine that for yourself. You set the pace, you make out the skeleton, and nature will fill in the meat on the bones. But you certainly have to lay out the blueprint of the skeleton of the thing that you want in life. That is your prerogative and also your responsibility.

I will tell you another thing about this great blessing we have of being able to control our minds entirely. Nature sends over with that blessing two sealed envelopes. In one is a long list of the penalties you have to pay if you neglect to use that blessing, and the list is long, believe you me, and in the other sealed envelope there is a list of the blessings you will enjoy if you do act upon that great gift of the Creator, and that list is also long. It constitutes everything in life that you could wish for, and the difference between failure and success depends entirely upon whether you use this power to control your mind for the things you want or allow it to go wild and attract to you the things you don't want.

Commentator:

Thank you, Dr. Napoleon Hill. Tune in next time, ladies and gentlemen, when Dr. Hill will explain the Mastermind principle, the second of his Big Five success principles.

FIVE
PERFECT HARMONY

Dr. Hill:

How do you do, my friends? May I share with you tonight another of the Big Five Principles of Success, which have helped thousands of people to find health, wealth, and peace of mind? In our last program, we described the first of the Big Five principles, Definiteness of Purpose. We come now to the second of these principles, which is the Mastermind principle.

Commentator:

Dr. Hill, I suggest that you give our listening audience a clear definition of the Mastermind principle since this principle is seldom understood or used except by those who have reached the higher brackets of personal achievement.

An Alliance

Dr. Hill:

The briefest definition I can give of the Mastermind principle is this: it consists of an alliance of two or more people working together in the spirit of perfect harmony for the attainment of a definite end. I wish to add that I have never known of great success in any business, industry, or profession that was not built upon the Mastermind principle.

Commentator:

Well, I notice that you emphasize two words in your definition of the Mastermind principle, "perfect harmony." Will you tell us what significance those two words have?

Dr. Hill:

Yes, and I am glad you asked that question because perfect harmony is the factor that distinguishes the Mastermind principle from ordinary cooperation. Now, let me give you an example of what I mean. In the great R. G. LeTourneau industrial plant at Toccoa, Georgia, I spent a year and a half training the two thousand employees in the usage and application of the seventeen principles of success. The Mastermind principle was so greatly emphasized that it had the effect of causing the management and workers to lay aside all motives of selfishness and pull together in a friendly spirit that took on the nature of religious zeal. The results were amazing. Production costs dropped to an all-time low. Gripes and personal complaints vanished entirely, and, strangest of all, the health of the employees began to improve so that the doctor was seldom needed. Compare these results with those experienced in the typical industrial plant where cooperation prevails, and you will get an idea of the power of the Mastermind.

Commentator:

Yes, I see clearly what you mean. When people associate themselves as you suggest using the Mastermind principle, they seem to tap an unlimited spiritual power. Now, Dr. Hill, will you turn back the pages of your book of experience and describe some of the results that have been attained by the use of the Mastermind principle?

Dr. Hill:

Well, let us start with my first experience with the "Mastermind," when I first heard of that term. It was during my first interview with the great steelmaker and philanthropist Andrew Carnegie. When I asked Mr. Carnegie to tell me how he had accumulated his huge fortune, he replied that it had been the result of the efforts of some twenty men who made up his "Mastermind group." Then he described his Mastermind associates one by one and told me what each man did, what contribution each man made in helping Mr. Carnegie carry out the object of his major purpose in life, which was the making of steel. One man, for example, was his chief chemist. Another was his metallurgist, another was his financial manager, another his legal adviser, and another his general plant manager, directly in charge of all of his industrial workers. After Mr. Carnegie had described each of his Mastermind allies, he then astonished me with the statement "I personally know nothing about the making or marketing of steel. But these Mastermind allies of mine know all that is known about the making of steel. The products of our steel mills are entirely the result of our combined knowledge, experience, and education. My job," said Mr. Carnegie, "is that of keeping these associates of mine working together in a spirit of perfect harmony." And that was where I first heard those two words, "perfect harmony."

Commentator:

Did you get the full significance of those two words the very first time you heard them?

Dr. Hill:

No, they made no impression upon my mind at that time, but later on, when I began to examine the background and methods of some five hundred of the top-ranking successful men of America, I was impressed by the fact that the degree of success each man enjoyed was in almost perfect ratio to the extent he had developed perfect harmony between himself and his Mastermind associates.

A Young Soldier

Commentator:

Will you give us further examples of the application of the Mastermind as you have seen it in operation?

Dr. Hill:

Let me tell you about one of the most interesting and profitable usages I ever made of the Mastermind principle. The story began right after the close of World War I, when a young soldier who fought in the war came into my office. All he wanted, he said, was a place to sleep and something to eat. If I ever saw a man who was willing to settle with life for a penny, he was that man. So I accepted him as a challenge to my own ability to lift men from low places to high ones in the world. For two hours I worked on this young man until I caused him to raise his sights and aim not merely for a meal ticket but for wealth in great abundance.

Commentator:

Did he accumulate great wealth?

Dr. Hill:

Yes, he did. But first let me tell the story of how I went about applying the Mastermind in his case. I knew then, as I know now, that no one has the right to seek great wealth or anything else without giving something of an equivalent value in return. During my two-hour talk with this young ex-soldier, I took complete inventory of everything he had to give in return for great wealth, and you may be surprised when I tell you how very little that was. I discovered that during his army experience he had learned to cook, and prior to his entry into the army, he had successfully sold brushes from house to house. So I went to work with these two assets and forged them into a plan whereby the young man began selling aluminum cookware by a very unique method. He would go to a neighborhood, select the most suitable housewife, and induce her to invite her neighboring housewives to a free dinner, which the young man cooked on his special aluminum cookware. Then, after the meal was served, he made appointments with the guests to call at their homes and talk to them about purchasing his wares. He became so efficient at selling by this method that he sold to an average of 50 percent of all the guests who attended his dinners.

Commentator:

That sounds like an excellent idea, but will you tell us how this young man started? I assume he had no capital.

Dr. Hill:

First of all, I took him out to my home and provided him with a room and meals while he was getting started in business. Then I guaranteed payment for his first purchase of aluminum cookware. And, to give him the necessary personal appearance he needed as a salesman, I gave him permission to use my charge account at a local department store. I also let him have a small amount of pocket money, which he needed for carfares, et cetera. My total outlay before this young man was able to go ahead on his own was only a few hundred dollars.

Commentator:

Did you ever get back your investment in the young man?

Dr. Hill:

Well, sir, he remained in my house for about a month. Then he moved to another neighborhood, and I saw him only intermittently for the following year. After that, I heard nothing of him for three years, until one day he walked into my office and announced that he had come back to pay up for what I had done for him. He said, "I wish to pay back the money you advanced me. In addition thereto, I wish to give you a sum of money, of any amount that you need, as a token for my appreciation for what you did for me at the time when I had no right to such help from a mere stranger." Then he began to pull out his bank deposit books from his pocket. He must have had at least fifty different bank accounts in as many different cities. "How much do they all represent in money?" I inquired. "Well, a little over $4 million," he replied. And then, he handed me a check that he had signed in blank, payable to me. And he said, "Fill it out for whatever amount you wish, and I will see that it does not bounce."

Commentator:

I suppose you were generous with yourself when you filled in the amount.

Dr. Hill:

My first impulse was to hand him back his check and tell him I had already been repaid by discovering such an honest young man, but I recognized that he had come back to see me with the full intention of giving a dramatic demonstration of the power of the Mastermind principle I had so successfully used on his behalf. So I did not feel like taking the wind out of his sails by refusing to accept his money. I filled in the check for $10,000.

Commentator:

How in the world did one man accumulate so much money in four years merely by selling cookware?

Dr. Hill:

One man didn't do it. After he got his selling plan refined and working smoothly, he began to train other salesmen to do the same thing and put them out working at his direction. And I might add that he related himself to them under the powerful Mastermind principle. You may be interested in knowing that this same plan of marketing aluminum and stainless-steel cookware has been taken over and is now in use by more than a dozen large concerns throughout the United States. One of my present students has an organization of over three hundred men selling under this plan. Not one of his men earns less than $600 a month, some of them as high as $2,500 a month, so, you see, this Mastermind principle has no limitations as to the results that may be accomplished by its application.

A Young Mountain Boy

Commentator:

Would you have a word of advice for those who have business or family problems that disturb them? Problems that might be solved through the application of your famous Mastermind principle.

Dr. Hill:

Take my own case, for example, and you will get a clear idea of what an unknown young mountain boy can accomplish through the use of the minds and education and experience of others. When I was given the job of organizing the world's first philosophy of personal achievement based on the know-how of successful men, I was so ill prepared to fill the job that I barely knew the meaning of the word "philosophy." But thanks to Andrew Carnegie's Mastermind relationship with me, and through his help, I gained access to the storehouse of experience of more than five hundred of the most successful men this nation has ever produced, and to the knowledge these men had gained by the trial-and-error method. I had the privilege of giving the world a philosophy of personal achievement that is unbeatable and foolproof, and, with all due modesty, I may add that this selfsame philosophy may well become the force that will bring harmony out of hostility in this fear-stricken world.

The Old Farmer

Commentator:

Can you give us an illustration of how the Mastermind principle has been used in a family relationship as the means of solving family problems?

Dr. Hill:

Yes, I could give you hundreds of such illustrations. Let us take the example of a man by the name of Milo C. Jones, who owned a small farm near Fort Atkinson, Wisconsin. Mr. Jones managed, with the aid of his family, to eke out a modest living from his farm until he was past middle age, when he was stricken by double paralysis and totally disabled as far as the use of his hands was concerned. In fact, he could not move any of his limbs or turn himself over in bed.

Commentator:

You might say that, as a farmer, Mr. Jones became a total loss.

Dr. Hill:

From one viewpoint, yes. From another viewpoint, decidedly no. I must tell you that there is seldom any sort of human handicap that cannot be overcome with the aid of some combination of the seventeen principles of success. While Mr. Jones was lying there flat on his back, he discovered a stupendous source of riches he possessed but had not been using.

Commentator:

Discovered a gold mine on his farm or, perhaps, evidence of an oil well?

Dr. Hill:

Something vastly greater than oil wells or a gold mine. He discovered he had a mind that he could take possession of and that it could be successfully directed to the achievement of any desired purpose. Yes, while

Milo C. Jones was lying in bed thinking, he had revealed to himself the supreme secret of great achievement that we mentioned in our previous program. The revelation struck him so forcefully that he yelled for his family to assemble around his bed while he told them about it. "While I was lying here in bed," he began, "a great idea has come to me, an idea that will bring us fortune if you will supply the physical labor to help carry it out. Now, as you of course know, I can no longer work with my hands, but you have the necessary hands to do everything I tell you to do. First, I want you to go to work and plant every available acre of our ground with corn. Then I want you to begin breeding pigs, which you will feed with this corn. While these pigs are still young and tender, convert them into sausage and call it Little Pig Sausage. We will sell it at wholesale to merchants all over the country."

And that was the beginning, friends, of a great national business that spread all over the nation, and which is still in operation today under the name of Jones Farm, although Milo C. Jones has passed on to his next reward. His idea, which came to him as compensation for the great adversity that overtook him, made the Jones family richer than it needs to be. Thanks to that adversity plus the application of the Mastermind principle with the Jones family, that same farm on which the Jones family had previously made only a modest living had made a huge fortune. It was the same land, the same soil, the same acreage, but something was added that made that soil yield greater returns. And that something was the discovery of the supreme secret and the conversion of that secret into great riches through the application of the Mastermind principle.

It is strange, isn't it? People so often have to be cut down by misfortune before they discover the supreme secret of great success.

Mr. Edison

While I am speaking of good fortunes being discovered through adversity, I must tell you about a conversation I once had with the late Thomas Edison. I asked Mr. Edison if his deafness was not a great handicap to him. His reply was most revealing: "No, on the contrary, it is a great blessing because it forces me to learn to hear from within." And right here we are again, rubbing elbows with the supreme secret of great achievement. Mr. Edison went on to explain that his deafness enabled him to concentrate his mind on any given subject without the outside distraction of sounds, and laughingly he said, "It also saves me from having to listen to a lot of idle chatter from people who have nothing to say and say it too often and too loudly."

Benefits and Advantages

Commentator:

Nothing idle about Mr. Edison, I would say. Before closing today's program, Dr. Hill, will you sum up the major benefits and advantages of the Mastermind principle?

Dr. Hill:

Well, first, the Mastermind principle is the medium by which one may procure the full benefits of the experience, the training, the education, and the specialized knowledge of others as completely as if the minds of others were really one's own.

Second, an active alliance of two or more minds in a spirit of perfect harmony for the attainment of a definite major purpose stimulates each individual's mind to a higher degree of activity than that which is ordinarily experienced, and it prepares the way for the development of that state of mind known as faith.

Third, a Mastermind alliance properly conducted stimulates each mind in the alliance to move with greater enthusiasm, personal initiative, imagination, and self-reliance, far above that experienced by the individual when acting without such an alliance.

Fourth, to be effective, a Mastermind alliance must become and remain always active. Mere association of minds by mutual understanding is not enough. Mastermind allies meet together, move continuously, and then pursue a definite objective, and they must do so in the spirit of perfect harmony.

Fifth, it is a matter of established fact that all individual successes and all levels of achievement beyond that of mediocrity are attained by the application of the Mastermind principle and not by individual effort alone.

Sixth, there are two types of Mastermind alliances. One is an alliance for purely personal purposes consisting of one's closest friends, relatives, or religious associates, when no material gain is sought. The other is an alliance for business or professional purposes consisting of individuals who have a personal motive of a material or a financial nature connected with the object of their alliance.

Application and Examples

The modern railway system is a good example of the application to industry of the Mastermind principle. The American system of free enterprise is another example. This system is the envy of the world because it has raised the standard of living of the American people to the highest degree ever experienced by mankind. The United States Army, Navy, and Air Force, through their system of coordination of effort, are excellent examples of the power that may be available by application of the Mastermind principle. This power was exquisitely demonstrated in both world wars.

All these are examples of the application of the Mastermind principle for the attainment of material objectives. Now let us consider an example of the other type of application of the Mastermind principle, for the purpose of establishing peace and understanding among men and women.

I have reference to Jesus of Nazareth and his twelve disciples, who formed the first Mastermind alliance for this purpose of which I have found any record. I wish especially to call your attention to what happened to the leader of this Mastermind group when one of its members, Judas Iscariot, became disloyal and out of harmony with the group. It led to the major catastrophe of the Nazarene's life, and I have seen similar things happen in business Mastermind groups, where one or more of the members of the alliance becomes negative and disloyal.

Commentator:

We hope you have enjoyed tonight's broadcast about the Mastermind principle. Please join us next time, when Dr. Hill will further explain the importance of these essential Foundations for Success.

SIX

HARMONY OF MINDS

Dr. Hill:

Thank you for joining me tonight as we further explore the important Mastermind principle, one of the Big Five Foundations for Success.

Here is a good definition of the Mastermind. It is an alliance of two or more people working in harmony, perfect harmony, with a positive mental attitude for the attainment of a definite end. That definition sounds simple enough, but there is much more behind it than meets the ear and the eye.

Let me begin tonight's broadcast with an explanation of the five major premises that make up the Mastermind concept.

The Major Premises

When I was first introduced to Andrew Carnegie, the first question I asked him was to tell me, in as few words as he possibly could, to what he owed his fortune, and he then said, "My fortune is due entirely to the work of my Mastermind." And he said, "That Mastermind is not made up of any one mind; it's made up of more than twenty men, whose background, experience, education, temperament, and ability have been combined and blended and directed to a definite end in a spirit of perfect harmony, and that end is the making and the marketing of steel."

That was the first time in my life I'd ever heard of the Mastermind principle. And later on, as I commenced to contact other men of great achievement, I found out that there was no possibility of great achievement except by the application of the Mastermind principle. That is to say, unless you learn to connect your mind with the minds of other people, and use their education, their ability, their foresight, their temperament, and sometimes their capital, you will never get very far.

All these great business achievements, like General Motors, General Electric, and Commonwealth Edison are the results of Mastermind alliances, including the application and use of other people's money. The Mastermind principle is a medium from which one may procure the full benefits of the experience, training, education, and specialized knowledge of others of influence, just as completely as if their minds were in reality one's own.

For example, contemplate what happened in the life of Thomas A. Edison. He was discharged from elementary school before completing one year. He never went back to school again. He never knew anything about any of the sciences, yet he selected as his major purpose in life a calling that made it necessary for him to use practically all of the sciences.

He had to have technical ability, he had to have scientific training, he had to have a great variety of things, and yet he had none of those. What did he do about it? He did what every successful man does: undertakes something that's beyond the realm of his own achievement. He surrounded himself with men who did have that ability, men who did understand chemistry, men who did understand physics, and men who had the necessary training that he himself didn't possess. He told them what to do, and they showed him how to do it.

In every instance where you find a man of outstanding achievement in any field, you will find that he has been a success as a result of a Mastermind alliance of one sort or another.

In Minnesota they have the great Mayo brothers' clinic. It is probably the greatest medical clinic of its nature in the entire world, and the reason that it is great—there are many reasons for it, but one of the reasons is that they have there in that institution medical men with almost every conceivable type of special training. When they put a patient through there, he is looked over by all those men. Why, they know what's inside of him and what's outside of him. The Mayo brothers understand and use the Mastermind principle.

Through the experience and knowledge of the geologist, one may understand the structure of a river's path without any training in geology. And through the experience and knowledge of a chemist, one may make practical use of chemistry without being a trained chemist. A man may choose as his major object in life any purpose that he desires, and even though that purpose involves an education that he does not possess, he could easily bridge that deficiency by surrounding himself with people who do have that education. Through the knowledge and skill of scientists, technicians, physicians, and practical engineers, one may become a successful inventor.

So the first premise of the Mastermind principle is that its operation produces more knowledge than is contributed by its individual members.

The second premise of the Mastermind is this: an active alliance of two or more minds in a spirit of perfect harmony for the attainment of a common object stimulates each individual's mind to a higher degree of awareness than that which is ordinarily experienced and prepares the way for that state of mind known as faith.

If you ever have the experience of sitting down in what you might call a "bull session," or a roundtable session, to talk about any problem or subject, you will find that as the discussion goes on you learn more and more about that subject. Oftentimes, the man that will come forth with the most enlightening conversation on the subject will be the one that knows the least about it. The harmony of minds enables you and each individual mind to tune in on sources of information not available to you under any other circumstances. That Mastermind alliance stimulates the mind and jumps it up, steps it up, and you can tune it in on the ether, which perhaps connects your thinking brain with Infinite Intelligence. That is a theory that might even be a fact.

The third premise: a Mastermind alliance properly conducted stimulates each mind in the alliance to move with more enthusiasm, with personal initiative, with imagination, and with courage, to a degree far above that which the individual experiences when moving without such an alliance. And to have the right kind of Mastermind alliance, when the going is hard, and you have problems that you don't know how to solve, you just go around and get your Mastermind allies together and start talking about that problem. Start talking with a feeling that somewhere along in the conversation, somebody will come up with the answer. And you will be surprised, oftentimes, as to the person who does come up with the answer. It may be the one you least expect.

The fourth premise—a Mastermind alliance properly conducted stimulates each mind in the alliance to move with enthusiasm, personal initiative, imagination, and courage to a degree far above that which the individual experiences when moving without such an alliance. I repeat that because I want you to keep it in mind when selecting and working with your allies.

The fifth premise: to be effective, the Mastermind alliance must be active. It is not enough to form a group and say, "Well, we're going to get together and that's my Mastermind group." It must be active. The association of minds is not enough. They must engage in the pursuit of a definite purpose, and they must move with perfect harmony, and they must do it continuously. Without the factor of perfect harmony, the alliance may be nothing more than ordinary cooperation or a friendly coordination of effort, which is something vastly different from the Mastermind. The Mastermind gives one full access to the spiritual powers of the other members of that alliance. The spiritual powers, now, mind you.

The "Big Six"

A great number of years ago, I had the privilege of dining at the Chicago Athletic Club with the "Big Six" of Chicago. The Big Six were William Wrigley Jr.; J. B. Lasker, owner of the Lord and Thomas Advertising Agency; Mr. Rich and Mr. Hertz, who founded the Chicago Yellow Cab Company; Mr. McCulloch, who owned the Frank Parmelee Transfer Company in Chicago, the largest of its kind in the world; and John R. Thompson, who owned a chain of stores.

All of these men started not too many years before I met them, without any capital whatsoever. They started meeting every Saturday night and going into a discussion of each man's definite major purpose. Each man had a definite object he wanted to attain. Nobody had any money. When I met them, the combined wealth of those six men was around $25 million. They had all become successful. They had become successful by lending their minds to one another. Their mental attitude was wrapped up in this principle of a Mastermind.

Astounding things can happen when two or more people get together and continuously meet and discuss the things they want to do. And incidentally, you as an individual may have one objective, and the man who is in the Mastermind alliance with you may have another. You don't have to have the same objective at all. But if you work together in the spirit of friendly harmony, you will find that you will get results.

The sixth premise: it is a matter of established record that all the individual successes based upon any kind of achievement, above mediocrity, are attained through the Mastermind principle and not by individual effort alone.

Most successes are the result of personal power, and personal power of sufficient proportion to enable one to rise above mediocrity.

It is not possible to obtain such power without the application of the Mastermind principle.

Roosevelt's First Administration

I had the privilege during Franklin D. Roosevelt's first administration of helping to build for the president and his administration the most astounding and outstanding Mastermind alliance this or any other nation has ever known. The object of that Mastermind alliance was to stop the stampede of people due to the Depression. Do you remember when Mr. Roosevelt went into office, shortly after that, they had to close down all of the banks because they were overdrawn and people were in such a state of fear that they had to do something drastic about it? We had to organize all of the public-opinion-molding machinery of the country and place it behind the president without bias, without prejudice, and without regard to political affiliation. And here are the six factors that made up that Mastermind alliance.

First of all, both houses of Congress, working in harmony with the president. For the first time in the history of this nation, we had both houses working tooth and nail in harmony with the president. They forgot about political bonds; they forgot about political expediencies. They became as one group behind the president of the United States. And the president of the United States, at that time, in that emergency, had no brand as a Democrat or Republican.

Second, the majority of the newspaper publishers in America. We induced them to take the scare headlines of business depressions out of the papers and to supplant them with the headlines of business recovery, to start talking about business recovery instead of business depression. We wrote appropriate news items for the newspapers and sent them out throughout the country, and as far as I know, no paper ever refused to print exactly what we sent out.

Third, the radio station operators of the country. They were sent material to use, and they used it just as it was sent. They got behind the idea of business recovery. They got behind the president.

Fourth, the churches of all denominations. That was one of the most beautiful things, ladies and gentlemen, that I have hoped to see in all my life. Catholics, Protestants, Jews, and Gentiles, all getting behind the president of the United States, forgetting for the time being whether they were Catholics or Protestants, whether they were Jews or Gentiles. It was one of the most magnificent things I have ever witnessed.

Fifth, leaders of both major political parties. These leaders of political parties, for the first time in the history of this nation, rallied to get behind the president. They didn't stop to question whether he was a Democrat or whether he was a Republican, or whether he was one of their party or not, they got behind him 100 percent. They stayed behind him long enough to get the Depression stopped and to get the stampede stopped.

And, of course, the most magnificent thing of all, perhaps . . . number six. Sixth: a majority of the American people, of all political and religious groups, rank and file. And how did we get to those American people? Why, we got through to them by those five public opinion sources that I just mentioned, especially the radio stations and the newspapers and the pulpit. Had it not been for the organization of the machinery of public opinion under the Mastermind principle, I am telling you that the results Mr. Roosevelt got in his first administration never would have been obtained.

Here was an alliance of many millions of people, which, in the aggregate, produced power such as this nation had never observed previously, and it was sufficient to stop the national stampede of fear and to avert what might have otherwise become a national catastrophe or a rebellion of the people.

The Right Contacts

Andrew Carnegie and his industrial staff, consisting of more than twenty business associates, formed the most outstanding and the most effective business Mastermind alliance I have ever known. I found that same principle obtained all the way down, through all the experiences that I have ever had with men throughout the country. The men who were succeeding in the best way had the brains, personality, and influence of other people. They had the right contacts. "The right contacts," ladies and gentlemen, is a great phrase. Did you know if you have the right contacts, you can do anything you want?

From banking, business, industry, or in almost every line of life, I have contacts all over the United States and, to some extent, all over the world, from which I can get things done for my students.

For instance, one of my students flew over here from India three or four years ago. He was here for six days, and during those six days, without my going out of my study, by using the telephone, I made contacts with the institute of the DuPont company, the Commonwealth Edison company, and with a great number of other companies, which enabled him to get enough orders and contacts for the sale of material produced in India, which would enable him to do a $2 million business here the following year. I didn't move out of my house to do it. He paid me a fee of $2,500, which I thought was high, but he said it was very low considering the results he got. And I didn't spend over $250 all told for telephoning. I couldn't have gotten those results if I hadn't known people in all those places where I was telephoning.

Contacts—having somebody at the right time to come to the front and do something for you is a perfectly marvelous thing, and no matter who you are and what business you are in, it is up to you; it's your responsibility to make contacts, friendly contacts, especially in the banks. You never know when you will need something down at the bank. Have a contact there, someone who knows you. It's surprising what you can do through contacts.

Forming an Alliance

As I told you last time, there are two general tracks of the Mastermind alliance. Number one: alliances for truly social or personal reasons consisting of one's relatives, friends, and religious advisers where no material gain is sought.

Number two: This is the other type of alliance that you probably will be interested in more, an alliance for business or professional advancement consisting of individuals who have a personal motive for material or financial success. There must be a motive. You can have no Mastermind alliance without every individual involved having a motive. You must be getting something out of it. You can't form a Mastermind alliance and use the brains, the experience, the friendship, and the love and affection, or maybe the capital, of another fellow without him getting something back from it. Even though he is willing to give his free time, don't you accept it; don't accept anything from anybody unless you are giving something of an equivalent value in return one way or another. Bear that in mind; just don't do it, because if you do, the relationship will play out sooner or later. I'll make this point over again. No one should receive favors from anybody without returning those favors. It's a good habit for anybody to follow.

Here are instructions for forming a Mastermind alliance.

First of all, adopt a definite major purpose with an objective to be attained by the alliance. Choose individual members whose education, experience, and influence are such as to make them of the greatest value in achieving the purpose. Be careful about those Mastermind allies when you go to choose them. If you happen to make a decision and get someone who doesn't fit, do the same thing as if you were in the apple business and you opened up a barrel and discovered a rotten one way down in the middle. It's a lot of trouble to get it out; you have to take out a lot of the ones that aren't rotten, but never stop until you get that rotten one out, because if you don't, it'll pollute all the rest. Don't have anybody in your Mastermind alliance who isn't in full accord with you and with everybody else in that alliance. If any two allies in your Mastermind alliance commence to be out of step with each other, get rid of one of them or both of them if necessary, and replace them with somebody who will work in harmony.

Two, determine what appropriate benefit each member may receive in return for his cooperation in the alliance and see that he gets it. Even though he doesn't ask for it, see that he gets it anyway. If he earns something, why, you know he earned it; you know the benefit of it, so don't cheat the other fellow just because of his ignorance. See that he gets everything he is entitled to and maybe a little more.

Three, establish a definite plan through which each member of your Mastermind alliance will make his contribution in working toward the achievement of the object of the alliance, and arrange a definite time and place for mutual discussion of the plan—a regular meeting time, a regular meeting place. Indefiniteness here will bring defeat. Keep a regular means of contact between all members of the alliance. These great corporations that are successful, these banking institutions, they have regular meetings of their Mastermind allies. They call them boards of directors. Well, an individual, just the same as a bank or an investment company, surrounds himself with a lot of people who can do things he can't do.

Mr. Carnegie dumbfounded me once by saying, "Don't ever do anything that you can get someone to do better than you can do." I thought that was kind of foolish when he first said it, but I found out later it wasn't. Mr. Carnegie also surprised me another way when he said, "These Mastermind allies that I have here are responsible entirely for my fortune. I personally don't know anything about either the making or the selling of steel, but in my Mastermind group there is all the

knowledge that there is about the making and the marketing of steel."
I said, "Well, what is your part, Mr. Carnegie?" He said, "I'm glad you
asked that question. You'll be surprised when I tell you what my part
of it is. My part is to keep these boys working together in the spirit
of harmony." I said, "Have you ever had to throw out any of your
Mastermind allies?" "In my entire life," said he, "only three." Three in
an entire lifetime.

Four, it is the burden of the leader of the alliance—that's you—to
see that harmony of purpose prevails with all members, and that action
is maintained constantly in carrying out the object of the plan adopted.
That's your major purpose.

And next, the watchwords behind the alliance should be "definiteness of plan and purpose backed continuously by perfect harmony."
The major strength of such an alliance consists of a perfect union of all
the minds of the members. Jealousy and conflict, as well as the lagging
of interest on the part of any member, will bring almost certain defeat.

Last but not least, the number of individuals in an alliance should
be governed entirely by the nature of the purpose to be attained. You
might need a dozen individuals or twenty, depending entirely upon
the nature of the objective and what has to be done in order to attain
it. That's your aim, to surround yourself with enough people who are
capable of doing things that you want to do, and maybe things that you
couldn't do yourself.

Commentator:

Thank you, Dr. Hill, for explaining the importance of a Mastermind
alliance and for telling us how it operates.

Ladies and gentlemen, join us for our next broadcast, when Dr.
Hill will begin his discussion of the third of the Big Five Foundations
for Success, Applied Faith.

SEVEN

A STATE OF MIND

Dr. Hill:

Greetings, my friends everywhere. We come now to success principle number three, and I sincerely hope that this broadcast will give you a better understanding of that mysterious power known as faith.

Let us begin by defining faith as a state of mind through which an individual may bring to pass any desired end or purpose as long as it is not in conflict with any of the natural laws. No amount of faith will cause water to flow uphill against the force of gravity, but faith applied to a definite purpose through the mind of an Edison can turn night into day by the mere turning of an electric switch. And faith applied to a definite purpose through the minds of Wilbur and Orville Wright can send carloads of freight sailing through the air to any desired destination with safety and great speed. And, what is still more important to each of you, faith can lift you from wherever you are to wherever you wish to be in this world. Faith can lead you to riches of whatever nature and proportion you may desire, and no matter who you are or what your education may be, faith can bring you sound physical health. Faith can remove the curse of any past mistakes you may have made, and if you happen to have been born under the wrong star, faith can correct that, too.

Commentator:

Dr. Hill, you have defined faith as a state of mind. Will you tell us how a person may go about creating the necessary state of mind? Is this something every individual can do for himself, or is it a gift only for the few who are more fortunate than the rest of us?

Dr. Hill:

Your question gives me an excellent position from which to take off in describing precisely how one may condition the mind for the expression of faith. Answering your question specifically, I would say yes, every person has the power to condition the mind for the expression of faith. Every person has this power because every person has been provided by the Creator with complete control over his own mind. In fact, this is the only thing over which any person has complete control. Here, once more, we are rubbing elbows with the supreme secret of all great achievements.

Absolute Control

Commentator:

Are we to infer from what you just said that every person, from the greatest to the most humble, has been provided with the means of absolute control over his own mind?

Dr. Hill:

Yes, that is absolutely true, and that's the reason why it is also true that whatever the mind can conceive and believe, the mind can achieve. This is no mere figure of speech. It is a great and profound truth. It is a truth the poet William Ernest Henley understood when he wrote those lines: "I am the master of my fate: I am the captain of my soul." Truly, every man is potentially the master of his own fate and the captain of his own soul because of the prerogative given him by the Creator, which gives him control over his own mind.

Right here is an appropriate place to call attention to another great truth in connection with the power of the mind, namely, the mind attracts to one that which it dwells upon.

Thoughts of poverty and failure bring poverty and failure just as unerringly as night follows day, and thoughts of opulence and plenty bring prosperity just as definitely. In other words, the mind attracts to one whatever the mind has been conditioned to attract.

Ten Thousand Failures

Commentator:

Do you mean that any person can condition his own mind to attract whatever he desires? If this is true, why do the vast majority of people go through life poverty-stricken and knowing nothing but failure and distress?

Dr. Hill:

The answer to your question should be obvious in view of what I have just stated, but let me explain it this way. The vast majority of people keep their mind trained on all the things they fear and do not want, such as the fear of poverty, the fear of ill health, the fear of criticism, the fear of the loss of love and affection of someone, and the fear of old age, and these fears have a strange way of materializing. People who have found the way to successful achievement keep their minds trained on things they do want, and by their thinking they condition their minds for the expression of that mysterious power known as faith.

Thomas A. Edison wanted to perfect a lamp that could be lighted and operated by electricity. He kept his mind trained on that desire through more than ten thousand failures while he was searching for a way to produce such a lamp. Think of that: ten thousand different failures and Edison's mind still kept on searching. The majority of people, especially those who do not know precisely what they want, would have quit trying after the first failure, let alone gone ahead in the face of ten thousand failures. And right here we are face-to-face with a major difference between an Edison and an average person. Edison discovered the supreme secret of great achievement. He learned how to apply it in conditioning his mind for the expression of faith, and then he knew the truth, that whatever the mind can conceive and believe, the mind can achieve.

I once asked Edison what he would have done if he had not found the secret of the incandescent electric lamp after having met with ten thousand failures, and he said, "Well, I would be in my laboratory right now searching for the answer instead of wasting my time out here talking with you." And he meant what he said.

Conditioning the Mind

Commentator:

Now, Dr. Hill, would you mind giving us a detailed description of just how one may go about the business of conditioning the mind for the expression of faith? You must have discovered a technique that works, and if so, it may be of great service to all of our listeners.

Dr. Hill:

Yes, I will gladly describe the steps necessary to condition the mind for the expression of faith, but first I wish to define further the real meaning of the term "faith." Faith is a mental attitude wherein the mind is cleared of all fears and doubts and directed toward the attainment of something definite through the aid of Infinite Intelligence. Faith is the means by which one may tap and draw upon the power of Infinite Intelligence at will. Faith is guidance from within, nothing more. It will not bring you that which you desire, but it will show you the path by which you may go after whatever you desire. Faith acts through the brain cells of the subconscious mind, the subconscious acting as the gateway between the conscious section of the mind and Infinite Intelligence. Keep that gateway open. Keep it free from self-imposed limitations, for Infinite Intelligence recognizes no limitations on the power of the mind except those imposed by an individual upon himself and those that would call for circumvention or suspension of natural laws.

Commentator:

Dr. Hill, is there not some reference to the Mastermind principle in the Bible, to the effect that "Wherever two or more people ask for a thing in my name, it shall be given"?

Dr. Hill:

That may not be the exact quotation, but yes, there are several such statements throughout the Bible, all of them clearly indicating that the power of an individual mind is greatly increased when it is blended with one or more other minds in the spirit of perfect harmony. And some believe that Jesus of Nazareth gained his powers from intimate association with his disciples. However, my personal knowledge of the power available due to the Mastermind principle has been gained entirely by personal experience and experimentation. And I have approached the study of this principle more from the viewpoint of the scientist than that of the religionist. This I do know, however: the Mastermind principle gives an individual great powers of thought control and thought guidance that he wouldn't have without it, and this conditions the mind for faith.

Commentator:

I believe we are ready now to have you describe the exact procedure by which one may condition his mind for the expression of faith.

Dr. Hill:

Well, the fundamentals of Applied Faith are these:

1. Definiteness of Purpose backed by a burning desire for its achievement and supported by continuous personal initiative and action. Remember, desire is the starting point of all human achievements, and the stronger the desire, the sooner it will burn away the negative influences of fear and self-imposed limitations.
2. A positive mental attitude must be maintained at all times on all subjects. The habit of indulging the mind in negative thinking even though it is only temporary would prolong the time necessary to condition the mind for the expression of faith.
3. You must form a Mastermind alliance with one or more people who radiate courage based upon a positive mental attitude. That is, people who are suited mentally and spiritually to one's needs in carrying out any desired definite purpose.
4. Recognize the truth that every adversity carries with it the seed of an equivalent benefit, and temporary defeat is not

failure unless and until it has been accepted as such. When overtaken by adversity, begin then and there to search for the seed of an equivalent benefit instead of grieving over the loss it may have caused.

5. Follow the habit of stating one's major definite purpose in the form of a prayer at least three times daily, especially just before going to sleep at night, and when you do so, see yourself mentally and spiritually already in possession of that which you desire. If you fail in this instruction, you fail in everything necessary for the expression of Applied Faith.

6. Recognize the existence of an Infinite Intelligence that gives orderliness to the entire universe, and recognize that you are a minute expression of that intelligence, and as such your mind has no limitations except those accepted or set up by you in your own mind.

7. Strict adherence at all times to the guidance of one's own conscience plus the habit of listening from within for its warning messages.

With each of these seven steps under your absolute control, you have the approach to mind conditioning that will prepare the way for the expression of Applied Faith. But remember, my friends, remember always that there is no such thing as something for nothing. Therefore, when you affirm your desires, do not neglect to also affirm the nature of that which you intend to give in return for that which you seek. There is some great force, both in the laws of mankind and in the laws of nature, that definitely frowns upon all endeavors to get something for nothing. Nature has no bargains. Her wares are clearly marked, and that price must be paid for everything one gets.

Maintaining a Positive Attitude

Commentator:

Dr. Hill, you have emphasized the importance of maintaining a positive attitude at all times on all subjects. Will you give us a few instructions on how one goes about the development and maintenance of a positive mental attitude, since this is such an important factor in conditioning the mind for the expression of faith?

Dr. Hill:

First, know what you desire. Decide what you have to give in return, which entitles you to receive it. Form a definite plan for going after what you desire, and work that plan for all you're worth. Take it to bed with you at night. Sleep on it, get up with it in the morning, and keep it in mind all day during spare moments.

Second, when you affirm the object of your desires through prayer, believe your prayers will be answered and see yourself already in possession of that for which you pray.

Third, keep your mind open always for guidance from within, and when you are inspired by hunches to move on some plan created by your imagination, which leads in the direction you desire, act upon that plan at once.

Fourth, when you are overtaken by defeat, as you may be many times, remember that people's faith is tested many times, and your defeat may be only one of your testing times. Therefore, accept defeat only as inspiration for greater efforts to carry on with the belief that you will succeed.

Fifth, keep your thoughts always on all the things and circumstances you desire and off all things and circumstances you do not desire, for thoughts are things, and they clothe themselves so they resemble precisely the material object to which you direct them—your desires.

Now, this last instruction is the most important. Keep your mind so busily occupied with thinking about that which you desire most that no time will be left for it to allow in negative thoughts concerning the things you do not want. If I repeated this great truth ten thousand times, that would be none too many. If you wish for success, you must devote yourself to success, and you must condition your mind to recognize it and to expect it and to demand it.

The Self-Confidence-Building Formula

Commentator:

Dr. Hill, I have heard that the majority of people suffer defeat all through their lives because they never have enough confidence in themselves. Does your experience prove this to be true, and if so how may one want to go about the development of self-reliance?

Dr. Hill:

That is a fine question, and I'm glad you asked it, for I shall now proceed to give you my famous self-confidence-building formula through which I have helped thousands of men and women take possession of their own minds and direct those minds to whatever goals they might have chosen. Here it is:

1. Adopt a major definite purpose, and begin at once to attain it using the instructions I gave in our broadcast on Definiteness of Purpose.
2. Associate behind your definite major purpose as many as possible of the nine basic motives.

3. Write out a list of all the benefits and advantages the attainment of your definite major purpose gives you, and call these into your mind many times daily, thereby making your mind success-conscious through auto-suggestion.

4. Associate as closely as possible with people who are in sympathy with you and with the object of your definite major purpose, and induce them to encourage you in every way possible. This has reference only to your close friends or Mastermind associates.

5. Let no single day pass without making at least one definite move toward the definite attainment of your major purpose. Let your daily watchword be action, action, action, and more action.

6. Choose some prosperous, self-reliant person as your pacesetter, and make up your mind not only to catch up with that person but to pass him with your own achievements. Do this silently without disclosing your plans to anyone.

7. Surround yourself with books of an inspirational nature, and with pictures, wall mottoes, and other suggestive evidence of self-reliance as it has been demonstrated by other people. Build an atmosphere of achievement around yourself.

8. Adopt the policy of never running away from disagreeable circumstances, but stand your ground and fight it out until you overcome them, and give no quarter whatsoever to procrastination.

Commentator:

It seems to me you have been very nearly describing a supreme secret of great achievement you have referred to so many times in these broadcasts.

Dr. Hill:

Yes, I have mentioned that secret at times on this and past broadcasts, and I will mention it in all future broadcasts. It is the way to health, wealth, and prosperity, including peace of mind. Have you in our audience discovered that secret?

Master Salesmen

Commentator:

Dr. Hill, you said something a little while ago about the nine basic motives that inspire all human action. Will you tell us, again, what these motives are?

Dr. Hill:

Yes, I shall be glad to describe them because one or more of these motives are responsible for everything one does or refrains from doing throughout one's life. No one ever does anything without a motive. Here are the nine basic motives. The first seven are positive:

1. The emotion of love, the highest and the greatest of all the motives for human action.
2. The emotion of sex, the great driving force for all creative endeavors and the means of perpetuation of every living thing. All good leaders learn the art of transmuting this great emotion into the achievement of their aims and purposes in life.
3. The desire for material wealth, an inborn desire because material wealth in reasonable and appropriate quantities is an essential for a person's life and goal attainment.

4. The desire for self-preservation.
5. The desire for freedom of body and mind, a motive of major importance that has been responsible for our great American way of life where individual freedom is every person's hope and every person's right.
6. The desire for personal expression and recognition.
7. The desire for the perpetuation of life after death.

Then come the two negative motives, which must be suppressed or transmuted to a positive end. And here they are:

8. The desire for revenge, for either real or imaginary grievances.
9. The emotion of fear.

All master salesmen understand and make use of these nine basic motives, which lead to action on the part of others. Master salesmen and great leaders, regardless of what they are endeavoring to achieve, never ask anyone to do anything at any time without having first established in that person's mind an adequate motive or motives for doing what is requested, and this is a pretty good rule for all of us to remember.

Faith Is Self-Attained

Commentator:

I have been impressed by the fact that not one of the prerequisites for the expression of faith you have mentioned is beyond the reach of the humblest person. And I have also been impressed by your emphasis on the point that faith is something one must attain for himself by his own efforts, not something that can be borrowed or purchased.

Dr. Hill:

Yes, faith is self-attained, or it is not achieved at all. It can be attained by the simple act of taking full possession of one's mind and directing that mind to the achievement of the desired ends. The giving of the power of faith is the Creator's method of compensating the individual for exercising his prerogative right to control and direct his own mind. Fear is a penalty imposed upon the individual for willfully or otherwise neglecting to take advantage of this great prerogative, whether that neglect is due to ignorance or indifference.

Commentator:

It has been said that the majority of all prayers go unanswered. What is your attitude on this question?

Dr. Hill:

It is true that the majority of prayers produce only negative results, but it is not true that these prayers are unanswered. The reason that most prayers produce negative results is that most people turn to prayer only at times of great stress, when their minds are upset by fear and anxiety. These states of mind bring nothing but negative results. The words uttered in prayer are unimportant; the mental attitude in which the words are spoken is everything. The mind that has been properly prepared for prayer always produces positive results.

A Properly Prepared Mind

Commentator:

Just what do you mean by a "properly prepared" mind?

Dr. Hill:

I mean that the mind begins with a definite desire, then intensifies that into belief in its attainment. Then it develops that belief through definite action, the same sort of action one would take if one knew in advance that this prayer will be answered in a positive manner. For example, when Thomas A. Edison tried one plan after another until he had undergone ten thousand failures while searching for the means of producing an incandescent electric lamp and did not once doubt he would find the answer, he was thereby uttering a prayer in a properly conditioned mind. A properly conditioned mind accepts temporary defeat only as an urge to further and greater action, and thereby throws itself in the lap of the power that operates this universe.

When I began publishing the *Golden Rule* magazine a good many years ago, just after the end of World War I, without operating capital, with full belief that I could make it pay, I thereby uttered a prayer of the highest order. The magazine earned over $3,000 for the first year, and I didn't learn until ten years later in a conversation with an experienced publisher that in order to start a national magazine with any assurance of making it a success, one must have $1 million in capital. How fortunate I did not know this in advance. By properly conditioning my mind, I went ahead in publishing my magazine in precisely the same way I would have proceeded if I had had the million dollars in the bank to begin with.

Commentator:

Oh yes, I see what you mean by putting action behind prayers. What about those timid souls who have been defeated so often that they have lost all capacity for belief in themselves? Now, how can they get back on the beam?

Dr. Hill:

I'll answer your question in full detail in future broadcasts, but right now I'll give you a clue that may help. When you face some problems that you cannot solve, and you've tried everything you can think of without results, there is always one thing you can do that may lead you out of the wilderness. Namely, look around until you find someone with a greater problem than your own, and start right where you stand to help him solve his problem, and, miracle of miracles, by the time you have helped your brother to solve his problem, the solution to your own will have come to you. "Help thy brother's boat across and lo! Thine own hath reached the shore."

Commentator:

Thank you, Dr. Hill, for opening our eyes to the importance of faith. Ladies and gentlemen, join us next time, when Dr. Hill will continue his discussion of this important Foundation for Success.

EIGHT

THE MAIN SPRING OF THE SOUL

Dr. Hill:

Welcome back, ladies and gentlemen. Let us continue our discussion of the vital role faith plays in achieving one's goals. In tonight's broadcast, I will explain the relationship between faith and one's mental attitude.

The Fundamentals

Faith is the state of mind that has been called "the main spring of the soul," through which one's aims, desires, plans, and purposes may be translated into their physical or financial equivalent. And the fundamentals of faith are these.

First, Definiteness of Purpose supported by personal initiative or action. There is no greater demonstration of the power of faith than to decide what you are going to do, to become determined in your own mind you're going to do it no matter how many things, how many people get in your way, or how long it takes, or what you have to pay to do it, and to carry out that plan whether the time is favorable or not. That's fundamental number one.

Don't do like the preacher who announced he was going to preach on Sunday morning for rain, and they all came down to hear this marvelous sermon, but nobody brought his umbrella. He said, "This is a heck of a fine audience. I'm going to preach on the power of prayer for securing rain, but nobody brings an umbrella. You might as well go home; the rain is not going to come if you don't believe it is coming."

There's a lot in that statement. You've got to learn to rely upon your belief, ladies and gentlemen. For instance, if you start out to make a million dollars, and you don't have ten cents, but you do have an objective and a plan for making it, you better make yourself believe you're going to make the million dollars or you're not going to do it.

A Free, Positive Mind

The next factor in the fundamentals of Applied Faith is to maintain a positive mind free from all negatives such as fear, envy, hatred, jealousy, and greed. Remember, your mental attitude determines the effectiveness of your faith, and remember also that mental attitude is the only thing in this world that you have control over. That is an astounding thing. It is an important thing in connection with this subject, and when you get to the point that you recognize this truth and begin to apply it, you will change the entire course of your life, you'll be able to obtain your objectives with less effort than you ever did before, and you'll be able to disabuse yourself of all sources of worry and fear.

An Alliance

Third, the next fundamental of faith is to develop and maintain a Mastermind alliance with one or more people who exhibit a mental attitude based upon faith and who are suited mentally and spiritually to one's needs in carrying out a given purpose. The reason for the building of that Mastermind made up of people who are suited mentally and spiritually to your needs is that the people you associate with have a mental attitude that is contagious, and you're bound to pick it up in spite of all you can do. If you could associate every day with a person who has perfect faith, who has a positive mind, you would have no trouble in accomplishing what you start out to do.

The Benefits of Adversity

And next, recognition of the fact that every adversity carries with it the seed of an equivalent benefit, and that temporary defeat is not failure until and unless it has been accepted as such. I think that is one of the most important things in the maintenance of Applied Faith. You must recognize that no matter how many adversities you meet with, or have ever met with, or ever shall meet with in the future, everything of that nature—every heartbreak, every hold back, every failure, every defeat, every adversity no matter what its nature may be—carries with it the seed of an equivalent benefit. If you are developing in your mind the power to use Applied Faith when these adversities or unpleasant circumstances come along, instead of groaning and moaning over them, instead of building your inferiority complexes as a result of them, you immediately start to look for that seed of an equivalent benefit.

Can you imagine having a nice house out here in the country, and you went out to the show one evening, and you left some very valuable diamond rings in the house, but while you were gone the house caught fire and burned down? When you got back, what do you suppose is the first thing you would start doing—looking at those ashes? What is the first thing you'd do? You know those valuable diamonds are in there somewhere in those ashes. Start digging for them, wouldn't you? You'd start stirring in those ashes of adversity to see if you couldn't find the one thing you could possibly redeem and bring out. And I don't care what your failure is, I don't care what your defeat is, it carries with it the seed of an equivalent benefit. The Creator never allows anything to be taken away from an individual without providing in the same circumstance something of equivalent or greater value to take its place, and that applies to the loss and death of your loved ones, which is perhaps the most unendurable loss you can imagine. Along with the loss of a loved one comes that potential possibility of the softening of your own heart, of your doing something for your own soul that you wouldn't have done without that grief.

Affirmation through Prayer

And next, the habit of affirming one's definite major purpose in the form of a prayer at least once daily. Use whatever form you please. If you have a certain ritual in connection with religion you use, do that so long as you connect with it the thing that constitutes your definite major purpose. Get in the habit of doing that. First thing you know you'll be thinking in terms of the things you can do and never think about the things you can't do.

When you want to do something, you'll know definitely that if you want to do it badly enough, you can always do it. One of my students asked me once, "What do you mean by badly enough—what is badly enough?" I wonder if you have ever thought about the importance of being able to think about things badly enough to be able to be sure to get them. Well, that's wanting them so badly that no matter what else may happen, you're going to put everything you have in life on the attainment of those things. Thinking about them, talking about them, feeling you are already in possession of them—that's wanting them badly enough. You must work yourself into a state of burning desire, and when you do that and place that behind a definite major purpose, that constitutes one of the finest prayers in the world, because it informs the Creator what you want, and it goes to the Creator with a picture of what you want in the right kind of order. If you go in with the wrong kind of mental attitude, you'll come back empty-handed no matter what form you pray in. You'll always come back empty-handed unless your mental attitude backs up the thing you go after, unless you believe you are going to get it, and you believe you are entitled to it and that you are determined to get it.

Recognition of Infinite Intelligence

The next fundamental factor of Applied Faith is recognition of the existence of Infinite Intelligence. The individual has a means of expression of this intelligence, and as such the individual has no limitations except those accepted or set up in his or her own mind. Now, I couldn't make that statement any stronger—that's as strong as the English language will permit me to make it. I can tell you now that if you follow this philosophy as I hope you will follow it, you will prove to yourself what I am going to say is true: that you have no limitations except those you set up in your own mind or permit the circumstances of life or the influences of other people to set up for you.

If you would examine yourselves carefully, you would find out that the limitations that have held you back in the past have been very largely, maybe entirely, the influences of other people. Or they have been due to the fact that you have been thinking in negative terms of fear. If you can rid yourself of those negative influences, if you could rid yourself of all the outside influences that are designed to break down your faith, the time will come when you can do anything you want to do.

Self-Respect

And next, self-respect expressed through harmony with one's own conscience. Ladies and gentlemen, unless you are on good terms with your own conscience, you'll never be able to make the fullest use of Applied Faith. The Creator very wisely set up your conscience as a judge advocate to whom you can go at all times to know what is right and what is wrong, and there is no one human being in this world who doesn't know at all times what is right and what is wrong unless he has choked off his own conscience and killed it by neglect. That's the one thing that will kill it off, so you do have to be on good terms with your conscience, and let it be the dictator.

There are times you'll have to make decisions as a result of your conscience that will be very unprofitable to you, but make them—go ahead and make them without any hesitation. If your conscience doesn't back you up, don't do it. If your conscience backs you up, go ahead and do it. Don't ask anybody, because you don't need to ask anybody. That's why the conscience is given to you, to guide you to make sure that you make no mistakes. The man that kills off his relationship with his conscience sooner or later comes into difficulty.

Creating a Mental Attitude Favorable for the Expression of Faith

To create a mental attitude favorable for the expression of faith, here are the things you should do, and incidentally your mental attitude is the lever, the pump handle, or the valve through which you control your power of faith. It's the only thing you do control.

To create a mental attitude favorable for the expression of faith, first know what you want and determine what you have to give in return for it. Know what you want; that's step number one in creating a positive mental attitude.

And next, when you affirm the object of your desires in prayer, let your imagination see your prayers fulfilled.

Third, keep your mind open for guidance from within, and when you are inspired by hunches to move on some plan that leads in the direction of the desire created by your imagination, accept the plan and act upon it at once. Don't neglect these hunches you get—they're rich with opportunity, richer than you may think. Sometimes you'll get a hunch that seems quite foolish because it leads you in a direction that you never thought you wanted to go. Neglect that hunch.

Remember always that there can be no such state of mind as faith without appropriate action. Faith without deeds is dead. There must be eternal action behind the things you go after, if you are going to make use of Applied Faith.

And next, when overtaken by defeat, as you may be many times, remember that man's faith is tested many times, and your defeat may be one of your testing times. Don't accept it as anything else. Therefore, accept defeat as an inspiration for greater effort, and carry on with the belief that you will succeed because you deserve to succeed, and if you don't believe you deserve to succeed before you start out, you might as well just stop.

And next, any negative state of mind will destroy the power of faith. Your state of mind is everything, and you alone control your state of mind. There may be times when the circumstances make it difficult for you to control your state of mind, as in the times of death of loved ones. It would be very difficult for you to control your emotions and not feel the pangs of sorrow—very difficult—but if you practice, you'll get to the point at which you can control your mental attitude at all times.

There are two kinds of things that people worry about that destroy their power of faith. One constitutes the kind of things that you can do something about if you wish to, and the other constitutes circumstances or things over which you have no control. Obviously, the latter should be dismissed from your mind entirely because you can do nothing about them. But for the former kind, the kind that you can do something about instead of worrying about them and becoming afraid and destroying your capacity for faith, the thing to do is to jump in and do something about them.

Next, a burning desire is the sort of material of which faith is created—a burning desire. When you have a definite major purpose and create a burning desire for the attainment of that purpose and do not back away from it, you bring it into your conscience many times a day, and you determine that you're going to carry out that purpose. That constitutes the finest application of faith you could imagine.

Mental attitude being the key to Applied Faith, let's see how many kinds of mental attitudes there are. Mental attitude consists of two kinds: the positive and negative. How can one control mental attitude? Well, there are many ways of controlling it: first, by exercising the power of will directed through Definiteness of Purpose based upon definite motives. If you give yourself a sufficient motive for wanting to attain an objective or do a certain thing, you will have no trouble in controlling your mental attitude in connection with that one thing. It depends entirely upon your motive, how badly you want to do it. If your motive is not strong, chances are you'll weaken when opposition comes along.

A Rich Garden Spot

Now, there are the nine basic motives I mentioned earlier, seven of which are positive, and some combination of those positive motives should be behind everything you start out to do, and the more of those motives you are activated by, the stronger will be your application of the power of faith. You can progress by keeping the mind charged with a burning desire for the attainment of definite objectives of a positive nature. Keep your mind charged at all times. Your mind is something like a rich garden spot. I can't think of a better analogy than this. And you have all perhaps lived at one time or another where there was a garden spot attached to the house or nearby, where the finest weeds on the farm would grow. You just didn't find weeds like them anywhere else, and also you didn't have to cultivate the weeds. Isn't that strange? You did have to cultivate the cabbages and tomatoes and other things, but not the weeds. You didn't even have to plant them—they planted themselves.

The mind is like that rich garden spot. If you don't plant in it the things you want to grow, and keep the things you don't want out, the things you don't want will take the place over just the same as they do in your garden spot. There's no two ways about it. It will work that way. You've got to keep your mind so busy doing and thinking about the things you want that it has no time whatsoever to sprout the seeds of weeds that will grow there without your effort and without your want.

I think that of all the sins of human beings, the greatest sin is that of idleness, allowing your mind to be idle, not doing anything at all, not working according to a plan. Avoid this by associating with people who inspire active engagement in positive purposes, and refuse to be influenced by negative people. In other words, choose the right people and avoid the wrong people.

A Mental Blind

It may be that you live in a house with some people who are the wrong people. Maybe your relationship with those people is such that you can't very well move out at this present time. Well, there is always something you can do. You can pull down the mental blind. I have a mental blind that I can pull down, and I don't see anything. I don't even see it if it is in front of me. And I have a set of mental earmuffs. I put it on my ears and I don't hear anything. I don't see anything, I don't smell anything, I don't taste anything, and I don't feel anything that I don't want to feel, or taste, or hear, or smell, or see. You can do that. You can be right near somebody that's negative and yet not allow him to have any of that negative attitude rub off on you.

How many times have I seen people whose elderly parents live with them or are so close to them that they had to be under their influence at all times? I had an experience of that kind one time, and I just simply shut out the part of their influence that I didn't want. I didn't allow it to make any impression upon me. They came into contact with me, but they made no impression upon me. I made use of that great law of passive resistance, which was the thing that enabled Mahatma Gandhi to free the Indian people from the British troops. He planted that idea in the minds of four hundred million of his fellow men, and they created the Mastermind there such as the world has never seen before, and that passive resistance did something to the British, and they pulled out without firing a gun or killing an Indian.

I'm talking about things you are familiar with. You may not be familiar with the reason or how Gandhi did it, but he did it by passive resistance, by refusing to accept the things he didn't want. If you stick to your guns, determined to do the thing you want to do no matter how hard the going may be—and you may be sure the going will be hard at first—lo and behold, you will come to the point sooner or later at which nature will say to you, "All right, old chap. You're a contrary cuss; I am spending too much time on you, so I am going over to this softy who cannot resist. You go on and take what you want. It's cheaper for me to get it to you than it is for me to fight you." Substantially, that's what nature says to you.

Complete Control of the Mind

And next, a profound recognition of the importance of the one prerogative of the Creator; that is, you possess complete control of the mind at all times if you will exercise that. Now then, how important is mental attitude? Judging from what I've just been saying, you'd say it is very important. I'll tell you it is the main control over the power of faith, but here are some specific indications of how important mental attitude is to Applied Faith. First of all, your mental attitude is the major factor that attracts people to you or can repel them. Did you ever think about that? Did you ever think that the people who are attracted are attracted to you not necessarily on account of what you do or on account of what you say, or on account of what you look like? They are attracted to you on account of what you think, and you don't have to express it orally, you only have to think it in their presence.

Of course, you just can't think a good thought in one's presence one time, and bad thoughts another time. A positive mental attitude that you express all the time reaches the people that you come into contact with, that you do business with, and it brings them back to do business with you over and over again. A bad attitude repels and keeps them away, and you wonder what happened to that man who used to come down and patronize you, and he never comes in here anymore. I didn't disabuse him, I didn't say anything out of the way to him, I treated him nicely, but if you would go back to the bottom of it all, you probably would find out that your mental attitude is not right. You were worried about something when you talked to him, you were out of step with somebody, maybe out of step with yourself or with your relationship with people.

And next, mental attitude is the major factor in the maintenance of sound health. Have you ever thought about that? It really is. You allow yourself to worry day in and day out and see how quick you come down with a cold or the flu, or something worse. Your body's resistance is destroyed by a negative mental attitude. A positive mental attitude supports and feeds that thing that nature has provided you to keep you well and healthy at all times. A positive mental attitude is the finest of all therapeutic agencies. All the doctors in the world cannot equal the importance of a positive mental attitude, and all of the better doctors of every school of therapeutics today recognize and make use of the necessity of helping the patient to maintain the right kind of mental attitude toward the doctor and toward himself, because you may be sure that the patient who does not have confidence in a doctor is not going to be benefited very much by that doctor, no matter how much he knows.

Cures take place not as a result of what the doctors do, but as a result of what the doctors get the patient to do himself. And that applies to financial cures just the same as to physical cures. The thing that would help you financially is not what I would teach you, not what I would say, not what I would write in books. The thing that would help you financially is what you do yourself. The attitude that you take toward yourself and that you take toward other people will determine your financial standing beyond any question of a doubt.

And next, positive mental attitude is perhaps (notice the wording of this) the determining factor as to what results you get from prayer.

And mental attitude is an important factor that determines whether you are a safe driver of an automobile or a traffic hazard endangering your life or the lives of others. Have you ever thought of that? Did you know that anytime you go onto the highway with an automobile steering wheel in your hand that that machine is a dangerous instrument if you're not in the right mental attitude? Did you know that? And you don't have to be drunk, either. You only have to be worried. Your mental attitude does control your driving. If you're not in the right frame of mind, if you don't feel right, you better just stay off the highway until you do.

I hardly need to tell you that if you are selling something, or if you are otherwise dealing with other people, if you are not in the right mental attitude, you just better stay away from them until you are. Stay away from them entirely no matter how much it costs you; stay away from them until you are in the right kind of mental attitude. You can do anything when you are in the right kind of mental attitude, and you can do nothing except that which is wrong when you are in the wrong mental attitude.

Next, your mental attitude is a determining factor as to whether you find peace of mind or go through life in a state of frustration and misery. You find peace of mind or go through life in a state of frustration according to the extent to which you control and maintain the kind of mental attitude you want. I don't know whether this impresses you the way it does me or not, but I think the most astounding thing in this whole universe consists of the fact that we know beyond a shadow of a doubt that the Creator gave men and women control over but one thing—not two things, but one thing—and that is his or her mental attitude. Surely, the Creator intended that to be the most important thing in the world, and it is, because if you control your mental attitude, you control everything else within the sphere of life you occupy. You are the dominating factor if you control your mental attitude. Yet the majority of people don't make any effort at trying to control their mental attitude. They get mad at a drop of the hat, and if a fellow doesn't drop the hat, they knock it off his head and then get mad.

And next, mental attitude is the very warp and woof of all salesmanship. Regardless of what you're selling—yourself, service, merchandise, politics, religion, law, medicine, chiropractic, or whatever you are doing—you're selling something. We are all salesmen. Some of us are not very good salesmen; we're very poor ones because we are selling in reverse gear instead of the third gear forward. Unless you condition your mind to make a sale, you'll never make one.

Somebody may buy something from you if he happens to need it and he can't get it anywhere else, but you may be sure you didn't have anything to do with making the sale unless you were in the right mental attitude when you were negotiating that sale. Doctors that have the greatest clientele are the doctors who maintain a positive mental attitude toward their patients at all times. I can assure you that oftentimes doctors get patients that are very difficult, and they try their capacity for self-discipline tremendously. There is nothing a doctor likes less than to get hold of a hypochondriac, someone suffering from an imaginary ailment, and yet the doctor must address himself to the hypochondriac just as pleasingly and just as pleasantly as if he were dealing with a truly sick person if he is going to have success in his profession.

A positive mental attitude is an important factor in connection with your entire station in life. The job you hold, the pay you receive, and the entire space you occupy in the world is dependent largely upon the mental attitude you maintain, and you'll never occupy very much space in the world unless that attitude is positive at all times. The man with the negative mental attitude occupies some space; he occupies just as little space, however, as people can get him into. They don't go out of their way to make space for him, you know that. Nobody likes a grouch, nobody likes a man who has something on his chest he wants to get off. Nobody likes a man who is disgruntled or has a gripe, or has mean things to say about other people.

Commentator:

Ladies and gentlemen, we have run out of time for tonight. We hope you have benefited from Dr. Hill's exposition on the importance of faith to achieving success, and on the interrelationship between faith and a positive mental attitude. Please join us next time, when Dr. Hill will begin his explanation of the fourth of the Big Five success principles, the importance of Going the Extra Mile.

NINE

THE LAW OF COMPENSATION

Dr. Hill:

Welcome, ladies and gentlemen. Tonight I will discuss the fourth foundation for success—Going the Extra Mile.

The Majority

Going the Extra Mile means the rendering of more and better service than one is paid to render, doing it in the proper mental attitude, and doing it all the time, and if you want to know the exact meaning of this principle, look around you, and I'll tell you it is just the opposite of what most people are doing throughout the world today.

The majority of people are not only not going the second mile, they are not going the first one if they can possibly get out of it. Looking for something for nothing never paid off; it never will pay off. It is unsound because it is out of step with nature's plan. Nature never intended for people to have something for nothing. You are only fooling yourself. You are getting something that will sour on you later. You will have to pay the price.

I am going to start off by giving you some of the reasons why you should go the extra mile in everything you do; why it pays to make it a policy, a habit, doing it regardless of what you get out of it. And I'll say in the beginning that you cannot go the extra mile without compensation. I'll give you a good illustration.

I was invited to speak to the Rotary Club today. I got no compensation out of it and didn't ask for anything. If I had delivered that same lecture to a business concern, they would have paid $500 for it at a minimum. I was glad to serve the Rotary Club, and after my speech was over, the manager of a Tennessee radio station came up and gave me his card, and also introduced me to the producer of the next program on that station. So it paid off double right on the spot. The law of compensation doesn't always work that rapidly, but in all instances you may be sure that when you render useful service in the right frame of mind, it will come back to you greatly multiplied, and it may not always come back from the source to which you rendered the services. It may come back from an entirely different source.

Fourteen Reasons

Here are some of the reasons why it pays to go the extra mile.

First of all, it places the law of increasing returns behind you. If it were not for the law of increasing returns, we would all starve to death in a matter of months. The farmer takes advantage of the law of increasing returns, you know. He plows the ground, he harrows it, he fertilizes it, and all of that costs money, but he gets something out of it. He has to do that in advance, and then he plants the seed in that soil at the right time of the year. He puts in a grain of wheat. He complies with nature's rules, all of which are summed up in Going the Extra Mile, and then nature takes over and brings him back that grain of wheat plus one hundred other grains to compensate for his efforts. If it were not for the fact that nature does work in this way, we would all starve to death. In other words, if the farmer put only one grain of wheat in the ground and got back one grain, there would be no percentages in that.

Nature recognizes the law of Going the Extra Mile in everything we do, and sees to it that we are compensated. There isn't a chance in this world of anybody doing anything to or for another person that isn't sooner or later done to or for him greatly multiplied. It works out that way throughout our lives.

Number two, it brings one to the favorable attention of those who can and do provide opportunities for self-promotion. I don't know of a single advantage that I have gained in life, that is a major advantage, that didn't come as a result of me going out of my way to do something for somebody else. I have never known an outstanding success in my life that didn't result from the habit of Going the Extra Mile, of rendering more service than I was expected to render and doing it in the right mental attitude.

Third, it begins to permit one to be indispensable in many different human relationships, and therefore enables one to command more than the average compensation. The fellow who goes the extra mile, if he is working for a salary or day wages or whatever he is working for, when times get bad and they have to let off others, the plant that is doing the employing never lets off the one who is Going the Extra Mile until the very last, and it doesn't let him off at all unless it has to do so. He is the one who has ensured himself a place. If there are opportunities being passed out, he has the choice of them; after all, he has earned them in advance.

Fourth, it leads to mental growth and physical perfection in various forms of service, thereby developing ability and skill in one's chosen vocation. I can truthfully say I have never delivered a lecture that I didn't intend to excel all other lectures on that subject that I've delivered in my life, and that doesn't have anything to do with the size of the audience or wherever it was delivered. I simply give the best that I have every time I do it, because in the giving of the best I become better than the next guy, and it is only by that means that I have advanced to the point where I can hold large audiences for as long a time as I choose.

Fifth, it protects one against the laws of employment and places one in the position to choose his own job and working conditions and to attract new self-promotion opportunities.

Sixth, it enables one to profit by the law of contrast, because the majority of people do not practice the habit but follow its opposite by trying to get more than they are entitled to. The law of contrast is a great thing. I remember having that brought to my attention once when I walked down in front of the Marshall Field & Company show window in Chicago. In one of these great show windows, there was a display of men's ties—nothing but men's ties—and in the center of this display was a dummy with a tie on. The tie was not straight, and it was not a good-looking tie. By the side of this dummy was a mirror, and when you walked up and looked at your own tie, the first thing you did was reach up there, and perhaps your own collar wasn't straight, and the tie didn't look just right. You said, "Well, my gosh, my tie doesn't look as good as those inside," so you walked in and bought a tie or a half-dozen ties. The law of contrast. The man who made that window was a psychologist. He knew that by contrast you would observe how much better the ties inside looked than the one you had on. It made it very easy for you to make that observation by placing that mirror there.

Seventh, Going the Extra Mile leads to the development of a positive mental attitude, which is among the more important traits of a pleasing personality. You can't adopt the habit, and follow it, of Going the Extra Mile without having a pleasing attitude toward other people. You just can't do it, and if you have a pleasing attitude toward others, they are going to reflect that same attitude back toward you. There are no questions of whether it works; you know that it will.

You can change your tone of voice in dealing with people so that you have changed the chemistry of their entire mind just a little by your voice. You can make them dislike you, you can make them like you, you can make them feel that they want to come back to see you again, or they hope they may never see you again, just by the tone of your voice, by the way you say things. Professionals who are dealing with clients should learn that, if you haven't already. They can multiply their patronage and their clients very greatly by the tone of voice in which they express themselves. They can cause those clients not only to come back again but to bring all of their friends and relations. People in businesses can do the same thing if they train those who come in contact with the public to properly moderate their voice.

Eighth, it tends to develop a keen, alert imagination because it is a habit that keeps one continuously seeking new and more efficient ways of rendering this service.

Ninth, it develops the important factor of personal initiative; that is, going out and doing things without somebody telling you to, without which no one may attain any position above mediocrity and acquire economic freedom. Personal initiative is the most outstanding trait of the typical successful American citizen, and this is a nation literally built upon personal initiative. Once you get in the habit of Going the Extra Mile, you find so many ways of creating opportunities for yourself, and one of the blessed things about it is that you don't have to ask anybody for the privilege of doing it. We can always find ways of doing something for somebody new without asking him whether we can do it. I never have yet asked, and if somebody is becoming offended or mad that I did something nice for them, I never have heard about it.

Why, you can even take your wife home a box of candy. You don't have to apologize, you don't have to ask her permission to do it, and no matter how long you have been married or how much you love each other, you would be surprised at how much she responds, the different look in her eyes when she kisses you. That's the difference. I don't have to describe that, and she responds, of course! You didn't have to do it; you've been married for years and she knew you meant to do it, but brother, don't take that for granted. Take that box of candy. Take that bunch of flowers. Take that extra ribbon she needed. Whatever it is—that little something. It is not the value; it is the fact that you thought in terms of your sweetheart. Keep on doing that!

I've been married to my wife for over ten years, and we're still sweethearts. I'm more of a sweetheart now than I ever was before, and that is because I found out how valuable she is to me and I don't want to lose her. I take her violets. I mean, I take her roses. Formerly, I might have taken her violets or something else. She gets the finest of things now. That indicates how much of a sensitive feeling I have toward her. "Dear Sweetheart" letters and all. We have a date almost every night. It costs a lot of money, but it's worth it. After all, she is the greatest thing in my life. She responds to my thoughtfulness. She wouldn't do that if I didn't go out of my way. And it pays off, and I am going to tell you, gentlemen, that it pays off handsomely. I have started courting my wife all over again. You can do it at any age; that's the beautiful part of it. Any age!

Tenth, it is definitely certain to develop self-reliance. It makes you feel good inside of your heart when you do something for another person that he wasn't expecting. There is something that happens to make you feel that. After all, you are just a little bit out of the ordinary— thoughtful and therefore self-reliant.

Eleventh, it serves to build the confidence of others in your integrity and general ability.

Twelfth, it aids you in overcoming the destructive habit of procrastination, which is among the most common causes of failure in all walks of life.

Thirteenth, it develops Definiteness of Purpose, without which nobody can hope for success.

Fourteenth, it is the only thing that gives one the right to ask for a promotion or more wages. See the significance of that? The majority of people who ask for a promotion or more wages give about every other reason except the only logical one, and the only one that is sound, which is the fact that they have already started Going the Extra Mile. That is the only thing that gives anybody the right to ask for more, because if you don't go the extra mile and if you don't render more services, then what are you being paid for? Then you are being paid for all you render. Aren't you? You haven't a leg to stand on.

The Laws of Action and Reaction

I remember an office boy. His name was Prudy; he once worked for me. He had on high knee pants when he worked for me, and one day he came in with long pants on about six months after he came to work for me, and he shouted up to me and said, "Mr. Hill, I would like to have more money now. What I am getting is not quite enough." "Well," I said, "Prudy, what have you done to entitle you to get more money?" "Well," he said, "it's not what I have done so much, but Mr. Hill, I have put on long pants now, and a man wearing long pants is supposed to be getting more wages." I said, "Prudy, that's a pretty slim reason, very slim reason for asking for a raise because you put on long pants."

A lot of men when they go to their bosses for a raise say, "Well, boss, I'm awful sorry to say anything to you about this, but after all my wife is going to have a baby. It's going to be more expensive, and I've just got to have the money." The boss would be real smart if he said, "That's all? I didn't have anything to do with that. It's your responsibility."

The point I'm making is that most people who look for advancement or look for a raise don't look in the right direction, and they don't create a condition that justifies them in looking, which is the fact that they should start Going the Extra Mile and do it for a sufficient length of time to let the employer know that they intend to keep it up.

Everywhere and in everything one may see the laws of action and reaction in operation, based upon this law of Going the Extra Mile. The pendulum swings back the same distance as it swings forward. The same is true in human relations and in the rendering of personal services, and you may put it down as an established fact that if you neglect to develop the principle of Going the Extra Mile, you will never become personally successful and you will never become financially independent. I couldn't make that any stronger if I preached it a hundred times, which is borne out by the fact that all people in the higher brackets of success follow this habit as an established part of their daily routine, in all human relationships, and not in just a part of them.

Wherever you find a man succeeding, you find a person who doesn't watch the clock. Whatever the job is, he has to do it in order to succeed. He does it regardless of how much time it takes or what effort it takes. He doesn't evaluate anything in this world so highly as his privilege of going out of his way to render useful service to other people.

Miracle of Miracles

One of the strange things about life, I think, perhaps the strangest of all the principles I have discovered during the building of this philosophy, is this: When you have a problem you can't solve, you have a dead-end street, you can't go any farther, you have done everything you know—and how many of us are there who haven't had such problems at one time or another? There is always one thing you can do that performs the miracle, and that is to look around until you find somebody else who has a problem as great or greater than yours and help the fellow solve his problem. Miracle of miracles, by the time you have found the solution to the other problem, the chances are that you have found the solution to your own. Why that is I haven't the slightest idea on this earth. I couldn't give you an opinion on it. I only know that that is the way it works out. I never let an opportunity go by to give help to some person who comes to my attention, and I don't care what the chances are of it ever benefiting me or not. I don't go into that. I don't even ask questions about it.

The Greatest Compensation

When opportunity takes a step into my path to be of service to another human being, I don't care if he is old or young, or if he is rich or poor. If it is within my power to render services to that other man, I always do it, and I have always noticed that the conclusion of that effort brings back the greatest compensation.

A little while ago, I was invited by a student of mine over in St. Louis, while I was living in St. Louis, to deliver a talk before the Chicago Rotary Club. Now, I hadn't the slightest reason to go to Chicago. It would take a lot of my time, and I'd pay my own expenses because a friend of mine wanted me to make a trip, and he was also a student of mine, and I said, "All right, Dr. Hancook, if it would help you, I will go." I went there in good faith and delivered the longest talk that I have ever delivered. It was two hours in the morning and two hours in the afternoon. I didn't know I was to speak all day, but I did. There happened to be in that group a dentist who had as his patient the son of W. Clement Stone, the president of a large insurance company in Chicago.

W. Clement Stone was a follower of mine. He had been a reader of my books for years and had taken a hundred dollars and a copy of *Think and Grow Rich*, and he had built that into a multimillion-dollar business in a matter of ten years. I did not then know Mr. Stone. When his son heard through the dentist that Napoleon Hill was to be on the program, he told his father about it, and his father came over and sat beside me. When the break came at luncheon, he said, "Mr. Hill, all of my life, ever since I have known about you"—he first told me of the tremendous success he had in the use of the philosophy—"I have wanted to translate your philosophy to moving pictures, and with your permission I can do so. I am in the position financially to do so. I'll do it, and I'll distribute those pictures throughout the country." I said, "All right, Mr. Stone, you can have that privilege."

Now Mr. Stone has formed a large and prosperous publishing and educational enterprise, all focused on spreading my philosophy of success.

Can you beat it? I say you can't. There is a lifetime of effort. There's a lifetime of opportunity, a lifetime of desire wrapped up in that one conversation, and I never would have met Clement Stone had it not been for going up there, because he thought I was dead. It was a great surprise when his son called him up and told him that Napoleon Hill was going to speak and would he like to see Napoleon Hill today.

The reason I am so enthusiastic about this subject is because it is a subject that most people pass over so lightly. Going the Extra Mile is one of the most vital success tools because you can always find means of using it without asking anybody's permission.

Paul Harris, when he got out of law school, wanted to build up a great professional association. So he started the Rotary Club of America. He invited in an important man from each industry, thereby making himself acquaintances in maybe forty or fifty industries. He built one of the greatest advertising enterprises of any man in Chicago, but he did more than that—he set up a force that now extends halfway across this world, all going back to the time when he went out of his way to render service to a group of men without pay. He formed himself a Mastermind alliance and had Definiteness of Purpose, and it brought Paul Harris greater returns in a matter of years than he could have expected otherwise in a matter of a lifetime. Incidentally, Paul Harris became one of the outstanding students of my success philosophy.

Commentator:

We have run out of broadcast time this evening, Dr. Hill. Thank you for your explanation of this important success principle, Going the Extra Mile. Ladies and gentlemen, please join us next time, when Dr. Hill will further educate us on the key role this principle plays as one of the Five Foundations for Success.

TEN

THE TRULY WISE BUSINESSMAN

Commentator:

Dr. Hill, I believe you are discussing again today the principle of Going the Extra Mile, so I am going to suggest that you select some of the very interesting cases in which you have used or observed this principle when it benefited everyone whom it affected. Friends, it gives me great pleasure to present Dr. Hill.

Dr. Hill:

How do you do, my friends, everywhere in this great and free country? And I sincerely mean it—it is good to be a free citizen of a great country such as ours, where everyone may become a king or a queen in his or her own self-chosen calling.

One Hundred Thousand Dollars

The story I am about to relate could have happened nowhere else on earth except here, so let us turn back the pages of the book of time to 1915, when I needed a working capital of $100,000. That was about $99,000 more than I possessed at the time. I needed the working capital to organize and operate a school of advertising and salesmanship in Chicago, and my problem was finding someone—other than a bank—who would finance me with only my experience and good character as security.

Commentator:

And were you successful in finding someone who was willing to invest so large a sum of money solely on experience and character?

Dr. Hill:

Do you remember in a previous broadcast, I said that whatever the mind can conceive and believe, the mind can achieve?

Commentator:

Yes, I do remember it, and it was a very impressive statement, even though it may be hard to accept for anyone with less experience than yourself.

Dr. Hill:

Yes, it was not hard for me to accept because I have made it lift me over obstacles that seemed insurmountable. I believed I would have the use of the $100,000 I needed, and that belief was translated into realization very swiftly. Before I give you the details, I wish to call your attention to the five principles of the philosophy of personal achievement I used in this transaction. Four of these we have described in this program up to the present, and the fifth will be presented shortly. They are:

1. Definiteness of Purpose
2. The Mastermind
3. Applied Faith
4. Going the Extra Mile
5. Creative Vision

These are known as the Big Five of the seventeen principles of success, and when they are applied by anyone who is in possession of the supreme secret of achievement, they carry an irresistible power.

A Financial Transfusion

You may be surprised to know that I chose, as the source from which I believed I would get the $100,000, a Chicago business college that had less actual cash than I personally possessed, but it did have a record of over fifty years of educational work and a good credit standing.

After my plan was worked out and ready to present, I called on the management of the business college and addressed them as follows: "Gentlemen, you have a college with a fine reputation, but at one time you owned over a score of such schools. Now all of them are gone except this one, and it is going down pretty fast. If you will permit me to do so, I'll give your school the same sort of financial transfusion that I gave the LaSalle Extension University, to the tune of over $1 million."

Commentator:

I thought you said you wished to get $100,000 from the school. Now you're talking about giving the school $1 million. That doesn't seem to make sense at all.

Dr. Hill:

Well, at this point, perhaps it doesn't make sense—but just wait until you hear the entire story, then tell me if it seems to make sense.

To get back to my story, I said to the business college management: "You, of course, know I have made an impressive record as advertising manager at the LaSalle Extension University, including procuring $1 million in working capital. What I propose to do for you is this: I shall join your staff as the teacher of a new course in advertising and salesmanship, and we will market the course both by home-study training and in local classes, with the advertising under your own name. This will serve a double purpose. First, it will put your name on the map throughout the nation, and, second, it will provide you with an income from this new course much greater than you are getting from all your other courses combined."

At this point the manager of the school spoke up. He said he was very much impressed by my plan, and from what he had heard of my record at the LaSalle school he believed I could carry it out successfully. But, said he: "Where do you come in? How much do you want for such a job?"

"Well," I told the manager, "if you ask how much salary do I wish, my answer is that I ask for no salary. My proposition is such that I shall take all the risk. I will do the job for you on this basis. You will use your credit to advertise and market the course. There will be enough tuition fees coming in from the local classes to pay the advertising bills as they become due each month. I will continue this arrangement until all advertising has been paid for and you have received $1,000 over and above that. This will give you the nation-wide stimulus of the advertising free of all cost, and $1,000 in cash. When I have accomplished this result, you will turn over to me the department of advertising and salesmanship, which I will accept in full payment for my services."

Commentator:

That sounds like a good deal to me, Dr. Hill. But I still don't see where the $100,000 you were seeking is coming from.

Dr. Hill:

Perhaps that is because you have not observed carefully enough. Don't you think that a going school with several thousand home-study students enrolled and paying tuition fees monthly might be worth even more than $100,000?

Commentator:

Oh yes, I'm beginning to catch on now. You built your school on the business college's credit, which made it unnecessary for you to have the $100,000 in actual cash.

Dr. Hill:

That's the answer exactly. But let us have no misunderstanding about one thing: I did not seek, and I did not get, something for nothing. The value of the work I did for that school was much greater than $100,000 because it saved the school from oblivion. It gave it a new lease on life. The last time I heard of it, that school was the ranking business school of Chicago, and in case you would like to know the name of the school, it was Bryant & Stratton College. The job took six months, so you might say that I gave six months of my time in return for the $100,000 I needed to start my own school. But mind you, I gave my services before trying to collect for them. Moreover, I made those services produce something of such a value to Bryant & Stratton College that I was entitled to receive what I got from it.

Application of the Big Five

Commentator:

Dr. Hill, will you analyze the application you made of the Big Five success principles in your deal with the business college?

Dr. Hill:

Well, obviously, my starting point was Definiteness of Purpose. I had to know what I wanted. I had to have a plan for getting it, and I had to find a source from which to get it. All of this required the use of the principle of Creative Vision, with which I assembled the other factors I have mentioned into a definite plan. In presenting that plan successfully, I had to condition it with Applied Faith to give it the necessary belief that the plan would work. Then I had to dress up my plan and give it appeal to provide the business college with a motive for accepting the plan. This I accomplished by Going the Extra Mile through six months of organized effort on behalf of the college. In the application of the principle of the Mastermind, I allied myself with other minds associated with the college, and we combined our resources of mind and our credit in such a manner that we got the use of the equivalent of $100,000 in advertising.

You can see very clearly that the omission of a single one of these five principles would have caused the plan to end in failure. And right here, I wish to remind you that whenever and wherever I am called in by an individual or a business firm to help solve any sort of a problem, I generally discover that the lack of a solution to the problem is due to neglect in the application of one or more of the Big Five principles.

Commentator:

You say that is true of individuals and firms who bring their problems to you, Dr. Hill, and it must be equally true of all other men and women who miss out on getting the things they really want in life. And as I understand you, each person can achieve what he wants if he will learn how and act upon what he learns. These principles that you call the Big Five must be recognized, and they must be applied. Overlooking just one of them may close the door to success and happiness—the door that has opened wide for so many who practice your philosophy. That's a part of your teaching, isn't it, Dr. Hill?

Dr. Hill:

Yes, it's a part of my teaching because I know that it's true, and I test it and prove it over and over and over again.

Neglected Principles

Commentator:

Now, Dr. Hill, I'm sure your listening audience would be interested in knowing which of the Big Five principles is most often omitted by those who come to you with unsolved problems.

Dr. Hill:

Generally speaking, the one that is most often neglected is the Mastermind principle. The successful business firms and individuals never omit the use of the Mastermind principle. They succeed because they have established alliances with a sufficient variety and number of minds to ensure an answer to any problem they meet with. How far do you think Henry Ford or Thomas A. Edison would have gotten with their definite purpose in life if they had tried to go it alone—without the brains and the experiences and the education of other men?

And the next of the Big Five principles that is most often omitted, especially by individuals who do not get ahead, is the principle of Going the Extra Mile. There simply is no method by which individuals without money and education and influence, people like Ford and Edison, can get a start beyond mediocrity without the habit of Going the Extra Mile.

Persistence and Endurance

Commentator:

Dr. Hill, to what extent do you extend your counsel to the person who comes to you for aid in achieving his or her major purpose in life?

Dr. Hill:

Well, sir, you'll be surprised, perhaps, when I tell you that once I take on a person for guidance, I'll never let go until that person is either soundly established on his path to his goal, or neglects to follow my instruction. Now, modesty may not be one of my ranking virtues, but persistence and endurance are, and it was because of those inborn traits that Andrew Carnegie commissioned me to organize a philosophy of success that he well knew would require both persistence and endurance for at least twenty years.

Commentator:

Speaking of persistence and endurance, would you mind telling us what you would have done if your plan had not been accepted by the Bryant & Stratton school?

Dr. Hill:

In view of what I have just said about persistence, I think the answer to your question is quite obvious. I would have promptly selected some other school, and had my plan not been accepted there, I would have selected still another, and another, and another, until I found the one that would accept and work with me. Just remember this: if it is right for a plan to be fulfilled, there is always a way to its fulfillment. I knew from the very beginning that the Bryant & Stratton school needed what I proposed to give it through my plan, and that knowledge was the major foundation stone on which I based my belief that the plan would be accepted. Students of my philosophy do not quit merely because they meet with temporary defeat. They make a new start and turn up the heat of persistence—just a little hotter. They know that a winner never quits, and a quitter never wins.

The Card

Commentator:

That's great philosophy. Would you mind telling us what are the first steps you take when a person becomes a member of one of your Mastermind personal counsel groups? Just what is required of that person?

Dr. Hill:

First of all, I must have a clear mental picture of every member of my Mastermind alliance. I must have a look at what goes on in his or her mind so I may know where to begin making corrections. The first thing a member is required to do is to fill out a card on which is set down a list of the things that this person must acquire in order to become a success from his or her viewpoint.

The questions on that card read as follows:

1. What is your major desire in life?
2. By what date do you desire to acquire it?
3. What will you give in return to entitle you to it?
4. What amount of money do you wish to accumulate for security and old age?
5. On the reverse side of this card, write down a briefly outlined list of everything else you desire.

At the bottom of that card is the following commitment, which must be signed:

> *"I believe that I now possess in my mind the things I have listed on this card, and I promise to carry out Napoleon Hill's instructions to the letter so that these things may come into my physical possession."*

Well-Organized Plans

Commentator:

Oh, I see. The things one desires must first be created in the person's own mind; then physical possession is gained by well-organized plans. Is that the idea, Dr. Hill?

Dr. Hill:

That's the idea precisely. I require every student of mine to give me a complete list of everything he or she demands of life, including the sort of house that is desired, its size, its location, and its furnishings; the sort of automobile or automobiles that may be desired; and the profession, job, or business in which one wishes to render the service necessary to earn the right to what is desired. And then I proceed to lay out the necessary plans for ensuring the attainment of those things precisely as I laid out my own plan for getting the $100,000 needed for my school.

Commentator:

Dr. Hill, your whole philosophy of achievement is rooted in a conviction that one must give to get. And the people who know and apply the seventeen principles of success as you define them not only advance their own financial physical and mental welfare but also strengthen the fabric of a whole society by joining with others in practicing this philosophy of self-reliance, straight thinking, and forceful action for success.

Dr. Hill:

That is absolutely correct, and I couldn't have stated it any better myself.

The Story of Charles M. Schwab

Commentator:

Dr. Hill, what is the background of the men and women who find success in your philosophy? Do many of them come from the ranks of labor?

Dr. Hill:

Yes, many of them, and I'm hoping and praying that the time will come—and very soon at that—when the philosophy of personal achievement will be written into every labor contract as the basis on which all labor will be performed. When this is done, there will be no more labor disputes, working men will be happy in their jobs, employers will be happy, and we the public, who pay all the costs of labor disputes, will also be happy.

Commentator:

I judge from what you have just said that you are not against labor unions. On the other hand, you desire to help all working men free themselves through the application of your seventeen principles of success. Now, isn't that the idea?

Dr. Hill:

That is precisely my idea, and it is the fruit of the seed planted in my mind by my sponsor, Andrew Carnegie, who helped more labor men to rise to positions of power and wealth than has any other industrialist. One of the Carnegie employees, Charles M. Schwab, started as a laborer at day wages. Through Mr. Carnegie's encouragement, Mr. Schwab adopted the habit of Going the Extra Mile, and by the use of that principle, almost exclusively, he became Carnegie's associate in business at a salary of $75,000 a year.

Commentator:

That was quite a jump from a day laborer's wages to an executive position at a salary as much as the president of the United States receives. What qualities made Mr. Schwab worth so much money?

Dr. Hill:

Well, the main thing that made him valuable was the fine, friendly spirit he spread among his fellow employees and business associates. You see, when a man forms the habit of Going the Extra Mile, he automatically spreads an atmosphere of good cheer wherever he goes, and this atmosphere is very contagious.

Commentator:

Did Mr. Schwab demand a salary of $75,000 a year, or did Mr. Carnegie pay him that amount voluntarily?

Dr. Hill:

It was a voluntary act on Mr. Carnegie's part, and that's not all. In addition to the $75,000 a year, Mr. Carnegie sometimes paid Mr. Schwab a bonus at the end of the year when business was good—as much as $1 million. You see, this thing called Going the Extra Mile has the power of dynamite when it comes to blasting the obstacles that stand in the way of personal achievement.

Commentator:

Yes, I would say it has the power of atomic energy. In other words, Charles M. Schwab received a salary of $75,000 for doing what he was expected to do, and sometimes received a bonus of more than ten times that amount for doing more than he was expected to do. Is that correct, Dr. Hill?

Intangible Benefits

Dr. Hill:

That's exactly correct, and I have seen it work out in a similar manner for many hundreds of my followers. But we have been speaking only of the benefits of Going the Extra Mile as measured in terms of money.

Let us not overlook the fact that the person who lives by this principle is free from stomach ulcers. He enjoys sound health, he is happy in his work, he is rich in true friendships that last throughout his lifetime, he is on good terms with his business or professional associates and colleagues, and he collects dividends of the business of life every day he lives. How do I know these things are true? Well, I know that because I live by the principle of Going the Extra Mile, and that is the only way you or anyone else will ever know of the great bounty of riches that come back to the person who lives by this principle.

Commentator:

But Dr. Hill, is it not true that sometimes people go the extra mile on behalf of selfish people who never respond in kind?

Dr. Hill:

Oh yes, that is true—that sometimes happens, of course—but the loser is not the one who renders the extra service, it's the person who receives the benefit of that service without expressing gratitude for having received it. Remember, whatever you do to or for another person, you do to or for yourself. The payoff of major importance for Going the Extra Mile is that which comes from within one's own mind. It does something to one's character in the way of building fortitude against disaster and defeat and adversity. It conditions one's mind to convert stumbling blocks into stepping-stones. The person who follows the habit of Going the Extra Mile at all times thereby reaches deep into his own soul and comes up with the necessary power to meet all the circumstances that affect his life. You see, there is something more than appears to the eye, something more than an increase in the bank account, which automatically comes to those who follow the habit of Going the Extra Mile.

The so-called smart businessman or professional man often squeezes the last penny out of every transaction, but the truly wise businessman follows a different policy. He goes the extra mile and thereby makes friends of his customers or clients, and the world makes a beaten path to his door. I know a groceryman, for example, who started his business only a few years ago in one small room, and now he has six great supermarkets in operation with thousands of customers daily. You'll be surprised, perhaps, when I tell you what very small detail helped this merchant to rise to success so rapidly. It was simply this: when his customer purchased, let us say, half a dozen eggs at seventy-five cents per dozen, he always threw off the odd half cent and charged only thirty-seven cents for the eggs. He was the only merchant I have ever known to do that. The others always add on a half cent and thereby buy themselves a half cent's worth of ill will, as a matter of fact.

If you stop to carefully analyze either success or failure, you will find that the final cause always consists of details so small that they are often overlooked. And they almost always involve Going the Extra Mile, when they result in success.

Commentator:

We have run out of time tonight, Dr. Hill. Thanks for enlightening us on this essential Foundation for Success. Folks, please tune in next time, when Dr. Hill will conclude his remarks on Going the Extra Mile, the fourth of the Big Five success principles.

ELEVEN

SOONER OR LATER

Dr. Hill:

My friends, may I give you this motto as a slogan for today's broadcast: "Render more services and better service than you are paid for, and sooner or later, you will be paid for more than you do." Today I am continuing with the fourth of the Big Five principles of success, which is the habit of Going the Extra Mile. Let us begin with a story I once heard Henry Ford tell, which accurately describes how the average person regards the habit of Going the Extra Mile.

Mr. Ford's Applicant

During the early portion of Mr. Ford's experience in building automobiles, he advertised for a man to fill a very important position. Several men applied, but one seemed to stand out well ahead of all others, so he was invited to have a talk with Mr. Ford personally. When they got around to the question of salary, Mr. Ford asked how much the man wanted.

"Well," he said, "all I can get."

They talked further, and then Mr. Ford said, "Well, I have no way of knowing how much you are worth, and you seem unwilling to set a figure, so let us arrange it this way: You go to work on this job for a month. By that time, we will become better acquainted with one another, and I will pay you all you are worth."

"Oh, no you will not!" exclaimed the applicant. "I am getting more than that where I am now."

Commentator:

I suppose the applicant didn't get the job, did he?

Dr. Hill:

Yes, he did. He got it, but he did not keep it. Mr. Ford talked him into taking it on those very terms. He said he learned long before the end of the month that the man had unwittingly told the truth, that he was getting more than he was worth where he had worked previously. You see, he was one of those fellows who believes the world owes him a living, and I doubt if he ever heard the truth, that the only way for one to get more than he is worth is by first rendering more service than he is being paid for, thereby making himself indispensable.

We have some interesting case histories showing what happens to men who make it a habit to go the extra mile. Yes, lots of them. Let us lead off with the story of the man who turned two sharpened pencil points into a $12 million fortune.

Commentator:

You don't mean that someone actually made $12 million by sharpening two pencil points, do you, Dr. Hill?

Dr. Hill:

No, I wouldn't state it just that way, but the two sharpened pencil points paved the way for an opportunity that paid off to the tune of $12 million. You see, if you carefully analyze the circumstances of both success and failure, you will find that they generally hinge on the very small details that most people never recognize.

Two Sharpened Pencil Points

Our story begins in the New York City bank where the founder of General Motors, William C. Durant, went one Saturday afternoon to cash a check. He arrived a few minutes too late. The doors had been closed, but he hammered on the door until the bank clerk opened it, and the check was cheerfully cashed. The young bank teller who opened the door and cashed the check was Carol Downs, who handled the situation so pleasantly that he attracted the special attention of Mr. Durant.

Commentator:

And what came out of the transaction?

Dr. Hill:

Well, sir, young Downs was invited to join the staff of Mr. Durant in a minor capacity, at a salary but slightly higher than he had been receiving in the bank. He accepted the job and was given a desk in the rear of a very large room where more than a score of people worked. At the end of his first day on the job, a gong was sounded at five o'clock in the afternoon, when all the other employees jumped and ran for the door, each one scrambling to be the first one out. Young Downs sat still, waiting—perhaps to keep from being stampeded by the dashing herd—until all the employees were gone. While he was sitting there meditating and wondering why everyone was in such a hurry to get away, Mr. Durant came out of his private office, looking as if he were searching for something.

"Can I be of help to you, Mr. Durant?" young Downs inquired.

"Why, yes," Durant replied. "I would like to have a pencil."

Downs took two pencils from his desk, walked over to a pencil sharpener on the wall, and put a neat point on each pencil, then handed them to Mr. Durant.

"Thanks," said Mr. Durant, and he turned around and walked back into his office.

Then, said Downs, "Mr. Durant turned around and looked me squarely in the eyes for a few seconds. Not a word was spoken, but something conveyed to me the thought that those two pencils had started a chain of events worth watching. As he continued, I made up my mind then and there that from that moment on I would never leave my desk until Mr. Durant left the office at the close of the day's work. I kept that up until Mr. Durant got into the habit of calling on me when he wanted something done. And the more I did for him outside of the regular line of my duties, the more I placed him under obligation to me."

Commentator:

In other words, young Downs was smart enough to stay on the job overtime because he recognized that the services he might render his employer under these circumstances would attract favorable attention to himself.

Dr. Hill:

That is the idea precisely. I hardly need to tell you that this is a far cry from the policy of the average employee.

Young Downs was transferred from one job to another for more than a year, probably to give him an opportunity to find out just where he fit into the picture to the best advantage. Then one day, to his great surprise, he was called into Mr. Durant's office and told that he had been chosen to go over to New Jersey and supervise the installation of machinery in a new automobile assembly plant the company had just bought. When Mr. Durant asked him if he thought he could do the work, he replied, "If you trust me to do the job, you may be sure I will do it, Mr. Durant."

"All right," said Mr. Durant. "The job is yours. It will take you about a month. When the work is done, come back and tell me how you're getting along."

Commentator:

That was a pretty risky assignment, was it not, Dr. Hill, sending a young ex-bank clerk to install costly machinery about which he apparently knew little or nothing?

Dr. Hill:

Under ordinary circumstances I would say yes, but young Downs was no ordinary person, a fact that Mr. Durant had obviously determined during the year the young man had been associated with him. Of course, you will want to know what was the first thing that young Downs did in carrying out his assignment. He did exactly what any student of mine would have done under the circumstances. He went out and hired an experienced engineer to go with him and help him install the machinery. He thereby made use of the principle of the Mastermind, which we discussed in previous broadcasts. Three weeks later, a full one week earlier than Mr. Durant thought the job would require, Downs reported back to the New York office. The job was finished.

Commentator:

What happened then?

Dr. Hill:

When he arrived at the office, he was told that Mr. Durant wished to speak with him immediately. As he entered Durant's office, Durant said, "Well, Downs, you have lost your job while you were away."

"I lost my job!" Downs exclaimed. "And for what cause, may I ask?"

"We will not discuss that just now," said Durant. "Go back and clean out your desk, then come back and talk with me. And by the way, you will see the new general manager's name on the glass door of a corner office as you go by." Well, imagine young Downs's surprise when he looked at that door and saw the sign that read, "Carol Downs, General Manager." He rushed back to Mr. Durant's office and asked the meaning of the sign.

"It means just what it says," Durant replied. "You have passed your final test in this company, and you have made the grade successfully, so you are now general manager, and your starting salary is $50,000 a year."

Commentator:

But what about the $12 million pencil point angle, Dr. Hill? It would take a man a long while to accumulate $12 million on a $50,000-a-year job.

Dr. Hill:

Of course it would, but Downs's salary was only a portion of his compensation. His association with the great industrialist threw him into contact with opportunity after opportunity to make money on the outside of his job. He developed these opportunities into a $12 million fortune, and right now he is retired and lives in Atlanta, Georgia, where he is still following the habit of Going the Extra Mile by serving as consultant to the Southern Governors' Association at the salary of a dollar a year.

Commentator:

Tell me something more about this man Downs. Was he a sort of genius, or did he have an unusually pleasing personality, or what was it that enabled him to find such a great opportunity in an office where his fellow employees were so busy running over one another to get away from opportunity at the close of the day's work?

Dr. Hill:

No, Downs was no genius, and he had just an average personality. But he did have one thing his fellow employees did not have, and that was a complete training in my philosophy of personal achievement. It was no mere accident that he placed two nice sharp points on those pencils. It was no accident that he gave Mr. Durant two pencils when he only asked for one. It was no mere accident that he thought of employing an experienced engineer to help him do a job he knew he could not do alone.

Commentator:

Oh, I see your point. Young Downs must have been a student of yours.

Dr. Hill:

Yes, and something more than a mere student. Once every week, from the first day he went to work for Mr. Durant, young Downs came to my office, and I gave him a step-by-step plan by which to relate himself to the job. And it was I who helped him find the engineer who installed the plant machinery. I did for Downs precisely what I shall do for you in my radio audience who hear what I say and act on it. You see, this philosophy of success provides one with absolute insurance against failure. That is, everyone except those who neglect to follow my instructions.

Commentator:

You say this philosophy provides one with absolute insurance against failure. In other words, it is a guarantee of success. Now, that is amazing. More so because to a lot of people the sort of success they want looks so far away, so difficult to achieve.

Dr. Hill:

The only thing one would have to do is to become a student of my philosophy and master the seventeen principles of achievement.

Established Confidence

Commentator:

Dr. Hill, will you give us some additional case histories of men and women who have become successful by Going the Extra Mile?

Dr. Hill:

When Mrs. Hill and I moved to California several years ago, we were sent into the Sixth Street and Grand Avenue branch of the California Bank with an introduction from a bank patron for the purpose of opening a checking account. The introduction was addressed to an executive of the bank. He glanced at the business card on which the introduction was written, tossed the card on his desk, and immediately proceeded to make out the necessary records for the account. While he was writing, I said something about the science of success philosophy. He stopped writing, picked up the introduction card again, and read it carefully. Then he discovered that I was Napoleon Hill, not just "Mr. Hill." He threw the card down, extended his hand, and said, "Oh, I thought you were just another Mr. Hill. Now that I realize you are Napoleon Hill, may I extend to you a special congratulation on having chosen the best city on earth, and the best bank on earth, and may I welcome you both. I want you to know that we are running the California banks on your philosophy and running them very successfully."

When we left the bank, we carried a letter of introduction to all branch California Banks instructing them to cash all checks that we might present. You see, the philosophy of personal achievement makes men and women achieve. It establishes confidence. It eliminates fear and suspicion. Yes, the California Banks are operated on the philosophy of personal achievement. That is one reason why they have the confidence of so many people.

Dr. Hill's First Position

Commentator:

Dr. Hill, would you mind giving some advice to young men and young women who are just out of school and wish to secure their first position? How can they make use of your success philosophy?

Dr. Hill:

Let me tell you about my first position, which I secured just after I had graduated from business college. That was several years ago, before I first met Andrew Carnegie and received from him the assignment to organize the world's first philosophy of personal achievement. I looked around and picked out the most important and richest and most prominent man in Virginia, where I resided at the time, and wrote him the following letter.

> *General Rufus A. Ayers*
> *Big Stone Gap, Virginia*
> *Dear General Ayres:*
> *I have just graduated from business college, and I have chosen you as my employer, because you are the most successful man in Virginia, and I feel I could learn more from you than I could learn from any other person. What I desire is to know how much you would charge me to let me work for you for six months, after which you will know whether or not you wish to retain me in your service. Whatever price I pay you during those six months, I will gladly accept after that time as my salary if you desire to keep me.*
> *Napoleon Hill*

In due time, I received this letter from General Ayers:

> *Dear Mr. Hill:*
> *Come on and go to work at once. I never heard of you before, but anyone with the self-reliance you expressed must have other qualities worthy of consideration.*
> *Yours truly,*
> *Rufus A. Ayers*

Commentator:

How very interesting. Will you tell us what happened after you received that letter?

Dr. Hill:

Yes, I went to work for General Ayers as his stenographer. Before the end of the first year, I was appointed general manager of the Seaboard Coal Company of Richlands, Virginia, owned by General Ayers, while I was still in my teens. And it was the record I made in this job, by applying the principle of Going the Extra Mile, that led eventually to my meeting with Andrew Carnegie, who gave me the greatest opportunity ever enjoyed by any writer: an opportunity to "go to school," to study five hundred successful men who helped me to organize the world's first philosophy of personal achievement.

Commentator:

In other words, you chose your own employer and approached him in such a way that he could not well refuse to give you a job. Is that the idea, Dr. Hill?

Dr. Hill:

Yes, and I have taught thousands of men and women to similarly choose their employers and get whatever positions in life they choose.

Late Rewards

Commentator:

I have a question to ask you, Dr. Hill. I have heard it said that you have made more successes than any other living person. This is an astounding statement, and while I have no doubt it is true, would you mind giving us a description of some of these cases?

Dr. Hill:

Certainly. Let us go back thirty-five years, when I was called in by the LaSalle Extension University of Chicago to help solve its major problem, consisting of its need for operating capital. Strangely enough, I found a solution where the school's officials had never thought of looking for it. I wrote a letter to the school's eighteen thousand students in which I sold them the idea of becoming partners in the school by purchasing stock. And then I followed through with another letter in which I induced the student stockholders to become salesmen for the school, by persuading their friends to enroll for its home-study courses. Within six months after I put the plan to work, the school received over $1 million from its students. Moreover, they more than doubled the school's enrollment, and, as far as I know, the plan I introduced is still in operation.

Commentator:

Did the plan pay off for you, Dr. Hill, as well as it did for the LaSalle school?

Dr. Hill:

Yes, I would say that in the long run it paid off even better for me than for the school, for it was responsible in the main for my having been appointed confidential adviser to President Woodrow Wilson during World War I. In that job, I made lifelong friendships of priceless value. Please remember this: anytime you render a useful service and do it in a pleasing manner, you are sure to be rewarded, although the rewards may sometimes be late in appearing.

Commentator:

I'm sorry to say that our time is up for this broadcast. Please join us next time, ladies and gentlemen, when Dr. Hill will begin his discussion of the fifth and last of the Big Five success principles, Creative Vision. You will learn why Dr. Hill considers it to be one of the Five Foundations for Success.

TWELVE

THE IMAGINATION

Dr. Hill:

Greetings, my friends everywhere. My goodwill greeting to all of you tonight is this: I wish for each of you that same feeling of gratitude I enjoy in serving you through these broadcasts.

Today we come to the fifth of the Big Five principles of personal achievement, which is Creative Vision, or highly organized and controlled imagination. There are two forms of imagination.

First, there is synthetic imagination, consisting of recognized ideas, concepts, plans, or facts arranged in a new combination. Basically, new things or ideas are rarely discovered. Nearly everything known to and used by modern organizations is only a combination of things that are old.

Second, there is Creative Vision, having its place in the subconscious section of the brain, where it serves as the medium by which basically new facts or ideas are revealed. One of the strange features of Creative Vision consists of the fact that it seldom operates unless it is quickened and inspired through a burning desire or some very definite and intense motive.

The Stimulant

Commentator:

Dr. Hill, do you have a technique or method by which an individual may stimulate his faculty of creative imagination into action at will?

Dr. Hill:

Oh yes, I do. That is accomplished through the application of the Mastermind principle. When two or more minds are blended in a state of perfect harmony and Definiteness of Purpose, the faculty of Creative Vision is stimulated in each individual, which enables him to connect with Infinite Intelligence. It is important that you take notice of this point because you will then better understand and appreciate the vast powers available to you through the Mastermind principle, which I have presented on previous programs.

If you are a student of the psychology of worship, you of course know the heights an individual mind may attain during a religious ceremony. You may be interested in knowing that any idea, desire, plan, or purpose you have brought into the conscious mind during these experiences of intensified emotion is automatically picked up by the subconscious section of the mind and carried out eventually to its logical conclusion by whatever natural means may be available to the individual.

Commentator:

How very interesting. I'm beginning to understand the significance of your description of the four previous principles of personal achievement you have presented on this program. They serve to condition the mind for the use of Creative Vision, do they not?

Dr. Hill:

Yes, sir. That's the idea exactly. When one combines the principles of Definiteness of Purpose, the Mastermind, Applied Faith, and Going the Extra Mile, the mind is then conditioned for the application of the principle of Creative Vision. The matter of conditioning one's mind for successful actions is a progressive act that is developed step by step through the seventeen principles of the science of success.

Mr. Edison's Invention

Commentator:

Perhaps the listening audience would like you to give us some examples of both synthetic imagination and Creative Vision.

Dr. Hill:

That's a very good idea and one that I can easily comply with. First, as an example of the use of synthetic imagination, let us take the case of Thomas A. Edison's invention of the incandescent electric lamp. I told you on a previous program that Edison failed in more than ten thousand separate experiments before he finally uncovered the two simple ideas that, when combined, gave the world its first incandescent electric lamp. He was using synthetic imagination, putting together old ideas in new ways. Then, almost by mere chance, Edison resorted to the use of Creative Vision and got the answer to his problem in a matter of minutes. He had spent another entire day searching for the answer when he became exhausted and lay down for one of those fifteen-minute catnaps for which he was so famous. Just as he awoke, the elusive thing for which he had been searching through ten thousand failures flashed into his mind. It consisted of one of the two factors that went into the building of the incandescent electric lamp. He had already discovered one of these factors; namely that by applying electrical energy to both ends of a wire, the wire would heat up until it made a light, but the trouble was that the wire would also burn up almost instantly.

Commentator:

Will you tell us, Dr. Hill, what was the elusive thing of which you speak that came to Mr. Edison's mind in such a mysterious manner?

Dr. Hill:

Well, sir, it was a very simple thing that had been known to man ever since the discovery of fire. It was the simple principle by which charcoal is produced—by setting a pile of wood on fire, covering it over with dirt, and allowing the heat to smolder until the wood slowly burns into what is known as charcoal. You know that where there is no oxygen, there can be no combustion. When there is but little oxygen, as in the case of that which percolates through the dirt, it slowly burns the wood into charcoal. When this thought flashed into Edison's mind, he rushed back to his laboratory, placed a bent piece of wire into a bottle, drew all of the air out, and sealed the bottle neck, then applied the electrical energy to the protruding ends of the wire, and lo! The world's first incandescent electric lamp was born. It was born of two simple ideas brought together in a new way. Naturally, the wire couldn't burn up quickly because no oxygen was reaching it; therefore, there was no combustion.

Commentator:

Dr. Hill, I can think of a dozen questions I would like to ask you at this point all at one time, but most important of these, I would like to know why Mr. Edison labored through ten thousand failures through the use of mere synthetic imagination instead of calling into action at once this faculty of Creative Vision?

Dr. Hill:

Yes, I thought of that question shortly after I first met Mr. Edison, over thirty-five years ago, and when I put the question to him, he laughed and said, "I didn't use Creative Vision sooner because I didn't know it existed." There you have the whole story in one simple, forthright sentence. He hadn't used Creative Vision because he had not yet discovered it, but from then on out, Edison began to put the law of Creative Vision to work, and it helped him uncover more of nature's secrets than had been uncovered by all of mankind up until that time.

At this point I will choose my words with caution, for we are rubbing elbows again with the supreme secret of personal achievement, which each audience member must discover for himself. I can give you this clue, however: the majority of my students who have discovered the supreme secret usually do so during my lecture on Creative Vision or while reading that lesson in my books.

How much do you suppose that idea Edison had revealed to himself through the law of Creative Vision has been worth to the world in actual increased wealth? It would overwhelm my own imaginative faculty to even hazard a guess, but the sum must be stupendous in proportion, for the invention of the incandescent electric lamp ushered in the great electrical age, which is an indispensable part of our entire system of economy. It has not only earned hundreds of billions of dollars in material riches and provided jobs to hundreds of thousands of people, but look what it has done to lighten the physical labor of all mankind. It is wondrous that when the great mind of humankind turns loose an idea in this world, it may become a part of the plan behind the entire universe.

The Stock Boy's Idea
Commentator:

Dr. Hill, what is the next inspiring story as to how imagination is used to achieve success?

Dr. Hill:

Well, there is a very interesting case of one of my students, who lifted himself to fame and wealth in a matter of months with the aid of synthetic imagination alone. The man to whom I refer is Clarence Saunders of Memphis, Tennessee. Clarence was working in a local grocery store, delivering groceries and helping to keep the shelves stocked. One day when he went out to lunch, he saw a long line of people waiting to serve themselves in a newly opened cafeteria, which was the first such eating place he'd ever seen.

Out of curiosity he got in the line, he filled his tray with food, and by the time he reached the cashier's desk an idea had flashed into his mind. He became so excited over his newly discovered idea that he left his lunch behind, rushed back to his place of employment, looked at his employer, and said, "Boss, I have just discovered an idea that will make us a million dollars. Let's turn this grocery store into a self-help store, where shoppers can come in and go behind the counter and stuff their baskets with food and then pay at the cashier's desk as they go out."

Commentator:

Did Clarence's boss accept the idea?

Dr. Hill:

He did not. He said, "Now look here, Clarence. I have told you before that your imagination would someday get you in trouble. Get this straight, you are employed here to deliver groceries, not to sell me million-dollar ideas that are not any good. Now I'm going to fire you." "Oh, no you're not," exclaimed Clarence, "because I quit." And quit he did. The next time the boss heard from Clarence, he had formed a self-help grocery store chain and had opened the first store with money loaned by men who understood the value of ideas. Four years later he sold his Piggly Wiggly stores and cleared a little over $4 million.

Commentator:

Clever boy, Clarence. A little over $1 million a year. Wow. Boy, that is a lot of money for one idea, isn't it, Dr. Hill?

Dr. Hill:

Yes, and the idea was not even created by Clarence Saunders. He merely borrowed it from the cafeteria plan of serving meals. You might say he just grabbed the idea in the cafeteria that day, dragged it across the street by the ears, and gave it a brand-new use in the grocery store business.

Commentator:

I suspect that Clarence's former boss had reason to regret his lack of ability to recognize sound ideas, did he not?

Dr. Hill:

Yes, I have heard that he once said that the short speech he made before firing Clarence cost him approximately $100,000 per word, as Clarence had intended to give his employer half the interest in his newly discovered plan.

Commentator:

I have heard that Clarence Saunders lost all the money he made from his Piggly Wiggly plan. How did that happen?

Dr. Hill:

I don't think it appropriate for us to say too much about how it happened, because I like to play up men's successes, not their failures. But I can offer this suggestion, that if Clarence Saunders had gone a step further and had discovered the law of Creative Vision sooner in life, he might not have lost his earnings from the Piggly Wiggly stores. He lost his fortune in the stock market, but just before he died he used Creative Vision to discover the supermarket "self-checkout" concept. Mr. Edison, too, made a huge fortune, but he did not part with it because he had discovered ways by which to protect himself and his fortune. He was a frugal man, not prone to extravagance or financial risk.

An Alliance with Mr. Ford

Henry Ford made use of the principle of synthetic imagination when he built his first "horseless carriage," known as an automobile. It consisted of a combination of the ideas of a horse-drawn buggy and a steam-propelled threshing machine. Both of these ideas were old, but Ford combined them in a new way and gave them the necessary refinements to produce a modern automobile, which has changed our entire American way of life. In his early career, Henry Ford made use of synthetic imagination only, but later on he had revealed to himself the law of Creative Vision as a result of his Mastermind alliances with his wife and some of his business associates.

Commentator:

Dr. Hill, I have heard that Henry Ford was one of your collaborators in the organization of the philosophy of personal achievement, from whom you received some of your most beneficial aid. Is that correct?

Dr. Hill:

Yes, it is correct, but the alliance was by no means one-sided. And while I don't broadcast this fact, the truth is that I was a great help to Mr. Ford, just as great as he was to me, because it was I who induced Mr. Ford to adopt his famous five-dollars-per-day minimum-wage scale. That turned out to be one of the most profitable decisions Mr. Ford ever made, although it shocked the entire industrial world at the time. You see, five dollars per day was just about double the then-prevailing daily rate scale for average workers. I think I might with reasonable modesty tell you I believe my books and personal influences were a strong factor in Mr. Ford's having discovered the law of Creative Vision. Creative Vision led him to double his wage scale, leading to increased productivity and profitability.

Commentator:

That is indeed interesting. Mr. Ford was related to you both as your teacher and as your student. It is little wonder that you are known as a man who has helped more people to achieve personal success than has any other living person, for you literally went to school to learn from many of the men who have helped to make our country great, powerful, and rich.

Dr. Hill:

Yes, I suspect there has never been another philosopher who had as much help from successful men as I've had, and I'm sincerely hoping and praying

151

and believing that the help these men so graciously gave me may be in turn passed on by me to millions of people who have not yet found themselves, in this chaotic world of fear and confusion.

Let me give you a few illustrations of the use of the law of Creative Vision combined with the principle of synthetic imagination. A good illustration is the case of Orville and Wilbur Wright, who built and flew the first flying machine. Previously, nobody had flown a flying machine, but the Wright brothers kept on experimenting with the application of synthetic imagination until at long last the law of Creative Vision was revealed to them. Then they built the machine in which they made their first flight, using aerodynamic insights previously undiscovered.

Incidentally, you may be interested to know that the phonograph, or "talking machine" as it was originally called, was the only invention that Thomas A. Edison ever created using only Creative Vision. All his other patented inventions were revealed through synthetic imagination or a combination of synthetic imagination and Creative Vision. The idea for the talking machine flashed into Edison's mind out of thin air. As he described it to me, he went to work right where he stood when the idea had come into his head and made a rough drawing of the first model produced. He built it, tried it out, and it worked on the very first trial.

Suggestions

Commentator:

Have you some suggestions for those who would like to develop their ability to use the law of Creative Vision?

Dr. Hill:

Oh yes, lots of them. First, get on good terms with your own conscience by following its dictates always. Then, stop selling yourself short and begin developing a belief in your own capacity to do anything you desire to do, and keep your mind so busily engaged in getting the things and creating the circumstances you want that it will have no time to worry about that which you do not want. Find out who you are, what you want from life, and what you have to give in return, and then back yourself with everything you have. Hone your imagination to a keen edge by keeping it everlastingly busy on something over which you can develop an obsessional desire—obsessional, that is, not merely hopeful wishing.

Be at least as good to your physical body as you are to your automobile by seeing that it gets the right sort of fuel and upkeep and the proper cleansing in the inside. Stop bothering yourself with fear and worry. While you keep your mind busy with something better than worry, then set aside a silent hour when you may be still and listen for guidance from the small voice that speaks from within. Thus, you may discover and appropriate the greatest of all powers, the power of Creative Vision. Creative Vision is not the product of hustle and bustle, fear and worry, and anxiety and grief; it is the product of meditation and silent prayer.

Let me give you some food for thought, which may well start a chain of events in your imagination that will eventually give you financial security for life. The world needs a system of human relations that will convert employers and employees into a relationship of partners. Can you supply such a system? It needs a system of public highways that will cut down the outrageous death rate through automobile accidents. Can you supply such a system?

Commentator:

Dr. Hill, can you give us some more illustrations of how one may make profitable use of the principles of imagination?

Dr. Hill:

Let us take the case of a young woman student of mine who formerly worked for the telephone company. She complained that her wages were not sufficient for her requirements, since she had the responsibility of rearing and educating two young sisters. A careful analysis of this woman's talents disclosed that she had a very attractive telephone voice. I helped her to set herself up as a telephone saleswoman and taught her how to qualify prospective buyers of life insurance, real estate, automobiles, sewing machines, women's clothing, and other items, and very shortly she had a dozen other women working for her through a battery of telephones she installed in her home. The last time I heard from her, she employed over fifty women in that capacity, and her annual income was so large that I was cautioned by her not to mention it.

A Guarantee

Commentator:

And now, one last question for tonight that I've wanted to ask you for some time. Can you guarantee you'll make a success of anyone who will follow your instructions?

Dr. Hill:

That is a question no one has ever asked me before, but I can answer it by telling you I have never known any student of mine that failed except by neglect to follow my instructions. I have the formula of success, which is as definite as the formula for water—H_2O. The formula consists of the seventeen principles of personal achievement and, most importantly, the Big Five I have mentioned in these broadcasts.

Commentator:

Our time is up for this broadcast, Dr. Hill. Ladies and gentlemen, please join us next time, when Dr. Hill will conclude this broadcast series and his explanation of the Big Five principles of success.

THIRTEEN
THE LAST BROADCAST

Commentator:

Welcome to Dr. Napoleon Hill's final radio broadcast here in Jackson on the Big Five success principles. Today's subject is the imagination, a key part of Creative Vision.

The Workshop

Dr. Hill:

Somebody has said that the imagination is the workshop wherein is fashioned the purpose of the brain and the ideas of the soul. I think that's a very good definition.

There are two kinds of imagination, as I told you last time. First, there's synthetic imagination, which consists of a combination of recognized old ideas, concepts, plans, or facts arranged in a new combination. With synthetic imagination, new things are rarely discovered. Nearly everything known to and used by modern civilization is a combination of concepts that are old. I think if I told you to give me a brand-new idea that was not made up of something that was old, you'd be hard put to do it. I think if I gave you a day in which to get it together, you still would be hard put to do it because there are very few new things in the whole world.

They tell me down at the Patent Office in Washington that it's the rarest thing in the world for them to get an application for a completely new idea. Every application that comes in there—and there are tens of thousands of them coming in—is a combination of old ideas put to a new use.

The second form of imagination is the creative imagination. That's something else again. It has at its base the subconscious section of the brain, and it serves as the medium by which basically new facts or ideas are revealed. Revealed from where? That's an interesting subject; we'll touch upon that before we get through with this lesson. Any idea, plan, or purpose that is brought into the conscious mind repeatedly, and supported by emotional feeling, is automatically picked up by the subconscious section of the brain and carried out to its logical conclusion by whatever natural means are practical and convenient. Understand this truth, and it will be clear as to why one should adopt and begin to carry out a definite major purpose.

Synthetic vs. Creative

Now I am going to give you some examples of both synthetic imagination and creative imagination. Henry Ford's combination of the horse-drawn buggy and the steam-propelled threshing machine, and his system of financing his business, constituted the application of a synthetic imagination from start to finish. Ford was going down the road one day—he lived on a farm—and he saw one of these old-fashioned threshing machine outfits, where the threshing machinery is hauled by the engine and the motor supplies the power. The engine was pulling the outfit down the road, and he then and there conceived the idea of a horseless buggy, and he went to work on it immediately. He didn't create anything new; he simply saw an old idea, and he thought he would give it a new usage. He also thought that instead of using steam he would use gasoline, and he started in to invent the internal combustion engine, which he finally completed.

Later on, when it came to financing his business, he engaged in the use of synthetic imagination and did one of the finest jobs that has ever been done in American industry. He financed his business by getting the money from the people who would use his product, that is to say, his distributors. They were the ones who would purchase his merchandise, they were the ones who would profit the most by it, and they were the ones who, in turn, had to put up the money—and they had to put it up in advance, or at least a part of it. As a result of that method of financing, he kept the control of the Ford Motor Company in the Ford family hands. He didn't go into the public market to get his financing and consequently did not lose control of his company. I've often wondered why more concerns do not finance themselves on that basis.

Now I'll give you some examples of creative imagination. To begin with, radar is a perfect example of creative imagination. I don't know in whose mind or minds it was created—perhaps in a great number of minds, perhaps in a Mastermind alliance—but radar is the result of creative imagination for the simple reason that it represents a force that was never known previously to mankind. The modern radio represents the use of creative imagination. It was made possible due primarily to the discovery of Lee de Forest in creating the tube necessary in radio outfits. The Wright brothers' flying machine is an excellent example of creative imagination. Nobody had ever flown before the Wright brothers. A great many people had tried it, but nobody had ever created a satisfactory heavier-than-air flying machine until the Wright brothers went in the air and did it.

Dr. Gates's Most Marvelous System

Now I want to give you an illustration that'll be interesting to you. Dr. Elmer R. Gates, one of my collaborators and one of my teachers, with whom I worked for three and a half years, had a most marvelous system of drawing directly upon his creative imagination. When I first met Dr. Gates—I was sent there to meet him by Mr. Carnegie—when I approached the door and went in, the secretary said: "I'm sorry, but you will not be able to see Dr. Gates until late in the afternoon. He is sitting for ideas." I said, "I beg your pardon?" She said, "He is sitting for ideas." I said, "And what is that?" "Well," she said, "it's too long a story for me to try to tell you in the first place. And I don't know myself exactly what it is, but I know he goes off into a soundproof room and is gone for hours and hours, and when he comes out, he has problems solved and he has new ideas. Ideas are born during this hour or two or three when he's sitting for ideas."

That intrigued me. I sat down and cooled my heels in his office for about three hours, and finally he came out. I told him what his secretary had said, and he said, "Oh, come back and I'll show you what it is. I'll tell you all about it." That was quite a compliment to me—that he would tell me all about what I then learned was such an amazing process.

We went back, and he had about a twelve-by-twelve-foot room, behind the walls of which he had placed sawdust and other material to give him a perfectly soundproof space. Inside that room there was a little wooden table, and on it a great stack of paper and some pencils, and right in front of the table was a switch so that he could shut the light on or off at will. When he wanted to create an idea, he charged his mind with a complete picture of the thing he wanted to create, and he went in there and sat in front of this table, turned off the light, shut off the sound, and waited for his creative imagination to begin to give him ideas. On one occasion when he turned on the light and started to write, he wrote for three hours, and at the end of that time when he examined his notes he found that he had the answer to a scientific problem that had been bothering scientists right down through the ages.

I said, "Dr. Gates, what is the source from which you get this information?" He said, "I don't know, frankly, what the source is, but

I suspect that when I tune in on the ether in that room, I am tuning in on the minds back down through the ages, to the thinking that has been registered in the ether. I'm also tuning in on the minds that are available today throughout the world, who are thinking in terms that I'm thinking, and I suppose there are people who would say that I'm tuning in on Infinite Intelligence, which is the source of all knowledge, which knows everything that has been, that is now, and ever will be. If that satisfies you, that is the best answer I can give you. All I know is that I can come into this room with a problem—I haven't the slightest idea what the solution is—and 95 percent of the time, I can come out within a matter of from five minutes to two hours with the answer."

I was lecturing at Harvard Business School to a group of young men and women some years later, before the principles of radio had been discovered and developed, and I said, "Just judging from what I saw in the laboratory of Dr. Elmer R. Gates, judging from what I saw in connection with the way that he used his mind so effectively, I would say that the ether here in this room is so sensitive and so charged with other thoughts and things that if we could tune in on them and we could hear other people talking, we could feel them thinking."

I looked around and I heard feet shuffling on the floor, and then I heard snickering. I looked at their faces and I saw them smiling, and then they burst into a horselaugh. They gave me a horselaugh! The idea of such a ridiculous thing as that. If I told you now that I'm speaking in competition with a band and a cowboy singer, and a hundred other radio programs that are available right here in this room, the noises are all here, you wouldn't laugh at me, you'd know it is true. You'd know that there is available here in the ether a great variety of influences that are coming from sources that we can determine. But what we don't know, ladies and gentlemen, is how many influences there are here in this room that are coming from sources we don't know anything about, and that the shrewdest men don't know anything about.

Marconi's Invention

Marconi's invention of wireless telegraphy is a fine illustration of Creative Vision. Nobody had done it before him. Edison's invention of the talking machine is another example. He conceived that idea, reached in his pocket, and got an envelope; drew a rough drawing of the machine that he thought he could carry it out with; and gave that drawing over to his patternmaker whom he told to make a pattern. In a matter of hours they had that pattern completed, and they tested the machine, and it worked the very first time they tested it. In other words, the idea came to him in pure form, unadulterated, and it's bound to have been through his creative imagination because nobody else, previous to Edison, had ever recorded and reproduced sound on any kind of a machine. He was the first one to do that.

The Big Five principles were necessary to make application of these illustrations I've just now given you. Creative Vision is needed in evaluating and preserving the great American way of life. We still enjoy the privilege of freedom in the richest and freest country known to mankind, but we need to use vision if we are to continue to enjoy these great blessings. Creative Vision and synthetic imagination are at an all-time low in this country, with reference to maintaining the things that we feel the proudest of.

A Look Back

Let us look back and see what traits of character have made our country great. First of all, the leaders who have been responsible for what we have in the American way of life made definite application of the seventeen principles of the science of success with emphasis upon these five:

1. Definiteness of Purpose
2. The Mastermind
3. Applied Faith
4. Going the Extra Mile
5. Creative Vision

And I would say that those are musts, ladies and gentlemen, in connection with practically all achievement that's worth mentioning. Those five are absolute musts. You might neglect or forget to use the other twelve principles, but you certainly could never forget and neglect these and hope to be successful.

The makers of the American way of life did not expect something for nothing. They did not regulate their working hours by the time clock. They assumed full responsibility for leadership even when the going was hard. And looking backward over the past fifty years of Creative Vision, I would say that the Wright brothers probably did more through their Creative Vision to change the habits of mankind than did any other person who lived during our present generation.

I would say that Andrew Carnegie, through his Creative Vision, ushered in the great steel age, revolutionized our entire industrial system, and made possible the birth of millions of industries that could not have existed without steel.

Looking backward over the past fifty years of development of the great American way of life, here is a brief bird's-eye view of what men and women with Creative Vision have given us: The automobile, which has practically changed our entire way of living. Airplanes, which travel faster than sound. Radio and television, which give us news of the world almost as fast as it happens. Electrical energy, which ushered in the push-button age, and radar, which gives us advance notice of approaching hazards. And by Creative Vision we have at long last uncovered the secret by which the energy of the atom has been released and harnessed for, we hope, the benefit of mankind. These are but a few of the astounding revelations that have been uncovered and added to the great American way of life by Creative Vision.

Commentator:

Thank you, Dr. Napoleon Hill, from all of us in Jackson, Mississippi, for spending time with us and sharing with us your science of success philosophy. You have brought hope to our community, and the tools to turn that hope into success.

A NOTE FROM THE NAPOLEON
HILL FOUNDATION

The Napoleon Hill Foundation was founded by Napoleon Hill and his wife, Annie Lou, in 1962 to perpetuate his teachings and spread his principles of success throughout the world. It is located on the campus of the University of Virginia's College at Wise, in Wise, Virginia. Napoleon was born in Wise County in 1883 and grew up in the town of Wise. It is here that the wild young man was influenced by his stepmother to trade in his six-shooter for a typewriter and to begin his career as an author.

Governed by a seven-person board of trustees, including Dr. Charles Johnson and Dr. J. B. Hill, Napoleon's nephew and grandson, respectively, the foundation has licensed Napoleon Hill's books in more than forty languages. It continues to license his classic books and to publish new books from original Hill material, such as the Jackson, Mississippi, radio programs appearing here. A not-for-profit organization, the foundation uses its revenues to teach Hill's principles in prisons, to provide courses and certification for teachers of these principles, and to grant scholarships and establish a professorship at the University of Virginia's College at Wise. It is currently cooperating with filmmakers who will produce movies based on Napoleon Hill's life and teachings.

For more information about the foundation, to sign up for free e-mail bulletins, or to purchase other books or recordings, visit naphill.org.

ABOUT THE AUTHOR

Born into poverty in southwest Virginia in 1883, Oliver Napoleon Hill was encouraged to write by his stepmother and soon discovered a talent for it. He began working as a "mountain reporter" for small-town newspapers and went on to become America's most beloved motivational author. His classic book *Think and Grow Rich* had sold twenty million copies by the time of Hill's death in 1970 and remains a cornerstone of the modern self-actualization movement. Before passing, Hill established the Napoleon Hill Foundation as a nonprofit educational institution, whose mission is to perpetuate his philosophy of leadership, self-motivation, and individual achievement.